D1575165

"'The heartfelt counsel of a friend is as sweet as perfume and incense,' says Proverbs. The wisdom available in this book bears just such an aroma, the pleasant fragrance of counsel dug from a life's worth of experience as a Christian leader. *The Tides of Life* is a written version of some of the things I learned from Bill Pollard as we worked together at Wheaton College, the value of which is marked by how often I find myself passing Bill's insights on to others. I highly recommend giving this book a close reading."

Duane Litfin, President Emeritus, Wheaton College

"This book is vintage Bill Pollard—full of intellectual challenge and ideas, affirming a strong faith yet not dogmatic, based on a lifetime of integrating faith and business while practicing servant leadership. A must for anyone in business."

Lord Griffiths of Fforestfach, Vice Chairman, Goldman Sachs International

"Bill has done a masterful job of translating the lessons he has learned in a lifetime of leadership in a manner that is easily understood and is actionable by any reader. The warm, personal stories of his life's journey, woven together as vivid pictures of leadership principles, make it real."

Don Soderquist, Former COO and Senior Vice Chairman, Walmart Stores, Inc.; Founder, The Soderquist Center for Leadership & Ethics

"Bill Pollard wonderfully shares a lifetime of experiences that help guide and counsel us about the importance of our choices and relationships as we confront a wildly unpredictable world."

Michael A. Volkema, Chairman, Herman Miller, Inc.

"My first meeting with Bill Pollard made a lasting impression. We discussed taking our Christian perspective in business to locations around the world that might not have an understanding or an acceptance of our faith. Bill shared with me his experiences in leading ServiceMaster as it expanded its business in the Far East. In *The Tides of Life*, Bill shares many inspiring lessons through his personal stories that will encourage us to choose to lead well in every circumstance— through joy and sorrow, success and failure. This is a book for those who desire to lead authentically and faithfully in the marketplace and in their personal lives."

Mary Andringa, President/CEO, Vermeer Corporation

"*The Tides of Life* is an excellent prescription for leadership written by a master practitioner of the art. Bill Pollard has been there and done that, and when he speaks, people listen. Invest in this book, read it; you will not regret it."

Josh Moody, Senior Pastor, College Church, Wheaton, Illinois; author, *Journey to Joy: The Psalms of Ascent*

"Life eventually takes us all in unexpected directions. One of my favorite sayings is 'If you want to make God laugh, just tell Him your plans!' *The Tides of Life* captures the critical importance of making wise and moral choices along the way. Bill's leadership insights and experiences integrating his faith into the ebb and flow of his own life will inspire you on your journey."

Bonnie Wurzbacher, Chief Resource Development Officer, World Vision, International; former Senior Vice President, The Coca-Cola Company

The Tides of Life

The
Tides
of Life

Learning to Lead and Serve as
You Navigate the Currents of Life

C. WILLIAM POLLARD

Foreword by Billy Graham

:: CROSSWAY

WHEATON, ILLINOIS

The Tides of Life: Learning to Lead and Serve as You Navigate the Currents of Life

Copyright © 2014 by C. William Pollard

Published by Crossway
       1300 Crescent Street
       Wheaton, Illinois 60187

All rights reserved. No part of this publication may be reproduced, stored in a retrieval system, or transmitted in any form by any means, electronic, mechanical, photocopy, recording, or otherwise, without the prior permission of the publisher, except as provided for by USA copyright law.

Cover Design: Erik Maldre
Cover Image: Property of author

First printing 2014

Printed in the United States of America

Unless otherwise indicated, Scripture quotations are from the ESV® Bible (*The Holy Bible, English Standard Version*®), copyright © 2001 by Crossway. 2011 Text Edition. Used by permission. All rights reserved.

Scripture quotations marked KJV are from the *King James Version* of the Bible.

Scripture references marked TLB are from *The Living Bible* © 1971. Used by permission of Tyndale House Publishers, Inc., Wheaton, IL 60189. All rights reserved.

Scripture quotations marked NASB are from *The New American Standard Bible*®. Copyright © The Lockman Foundation 1960, 1962, 1963, 1968, 1971, 1972, 1973, 1975, 1977, 1995. Used by permission.

Scripture references marked NIV are taken from The Holy Bible, New International Version®, NIV®. Copyright © 1973, 1978, 1984 by Biblica, Inc.™ Used by permission. All rights reserved worldwide.

Scripture references marked NRSV are from *The New Revised Standard Version*. Copyright © 1989 by the Division of Christian Education of the National Council of the Churches of Christ in the U.S.A. Published by Thomas Nelson, Inc. Used by permission of the National Council of the Churches of Christ in the U.S.A.

Unless otherwise indicated, photographs are the property of the author. Every effort has been made to identify and credit the rights holders for photographs and other images used in this book. Upon notice, the publisher will gladly correct any errors as quickly as possible.

Hardcover ISBN: 978-1-4335-4172-8
Mobipocket ISBN: 978-1-4335-4174-2
PDF ISBN: 978-1-4335-4173-5
ePub ISBN: 978-1-4335-4175-9

Library of Congress Cataloging-in-Publication Data
Pollard, C. William.
   The tides of life : learning to lead and serve as you navigate the currents of life / C. William Pollard ; foreword by Billy Graham.
      pages cm.
   Includes bibliographical references and index.
   ISBN 978-1-4335-4172-8 (hardcover)
   1. Pollard, C. William. 2. Business—Religious aspects—Christianity. 3. Leadership—Religious aspects—Christianity. 4. Businesspeople—Conduct of life. I. Title.
HF5388.P653   2014
261.8'5—dc23   2013040657

Crossway is a publishing ministry of Good News Publishers.

This book is dedicated to my wife, Judy,
who has been my partner for over fifty-five years,
and to our family, who include our children and
their spouses, and our grandchildren and their
spouses. I love you all.

Contents

)

Foreword

By Billy Graham

Leadership is a powerful force. Some use their leadership roles to control people. But many use this same influence to guide others, helping them to recognize the changing tides, encouraging them to respond in ways that move them in the right direction.

Those who master such skills are most respected when they are also great servants. Effective leaders are willing to invest themselves in others by passing on what they've learned. Worthwhile leadership has a powerful effect in a business, in a church, in a family, and in the life of one person at a time.

Such is the case with this book's author, who writes, "Leadership is an awesome responsibility." I would add that it is also a humbling privilege. Leaders are admired most when they exemplify strong character, depth of integrity, and a heart for others. This is the essence of my longtime friend Bill Pollard—a man who takes seriously the privilege and responsibility of authentic leadership.

With great clarity, Bill brushes the pages of this book with his own life's experiences, leading readers to recognize their own opportunities for leadership. When a leader serves others, he or she is mentoring them as they move with the tides of life. Without building on the bedrock of truths described in these pages founded in Scripture, changing tides can knock us off course. No matter what position a person may hold in life, until we each realize that life is about others and not ourselves, we will falter and miserably fail to impact those around us for good.

Bill Pollard writes about those who have invested in him. He shares from his heart how God has used others to shape his life and how it challenged him to do the same for others. While practicing law, Bill was sought by the president of Wheaton College, my friend Dr. Hudson Armerding, to join his team to lead and manage the business affairs and fund-raising efforts of the college. Among the things Bill and I share, Wheaton College is our alma mater.

After Bill's tenure there as vice president, he was persuaded through fervent prayer to join a company called ServiceMaster, run by another friend of mine, Ken Hansen. While a senior at Wheaton, Ken and I, along with some other fellow students, roomed together on campus at the Hansen home called the "Attic." So naturally I followed the growth of ServiceMaster with great interest.

When Bill was elected as the CEO of ServiceMaster some years later, he had learned the art of putting his faith into action in the workplace. Opportunities for service and leadership came through showing interest in others, helping others achieve what they might have never attempted.

I have often said that the marketplace may be one of the greatest untapped mission fields in the world, because people we work with weekly are in search of truth and authentic leadership. When a leader reaches out to others, people usually respond. Bill has been faithful to this mission and has made a difference as he has lived out the corporate objective at The ServiceMaster Company, as it was stated at the time: *To honor God in all we do.*

Bill writes warmly, but candidly, about his professional life and his personal life, giving great honor to Judy, his wife of fifty-five years. My late wife, Ruth, and I shared many wonderful times with the Pollards. One event stands out in my mind because it was just nine weeks after 9/11. Then President George W. Bush had the weight of the world on his shoulders. He served and led our nation during a tumultuous turning of the tide in America. Yet his mind was not on himself, but on others. My heart was deeply moved when the president and first lady extended a gracious invitation to spend my eighty-third birthday with them at the White House, inviting several of my family members and close friends to dinner. Bill and Judy were among those who sat with us as the president led in a moving prayer before the meal. We stood in awe as we observed how President and Mrs. Bush, with such grace and selflessness, opened their arms and hearts to us.

But Bill not only shared such memorable times with me in friendship, he has been a loyal adviser to me. While Bill has been recognized by Harvard Business School as an American leader of the twentieth century and has been honored in numerous ways, he has had a tremendous ministry impact while serving and giving leadership as chairman of the executive committee to the Billy Graham Evangelistic Association board of directors. He has mentored many wonderful people in our organization and has been a close personal friend—a confidant in our ministry affairs. Through the years, I have sought his counsel and we have prayed together for the Lord to lead our ministry work according to God's will.

While we have seen tides within the life of ministry shift, billow, and ebb, we have also seen that God's Word never changes. Someone has said: "Progress is a tide. If we stand still we will surely be drowned. To stay on the crest, we have to keep moving." While God's truths anchor believers in a changing world to stand strong and be bold, He will safely move us within the current if we will be faithful *to honor Him in all we do.*

This is what Bill is saying when he writes about learning to swim in an uneven world. Tides rise and fall. We can ride them or drown in them. But these tidal waters—always on the move—carry a depth of opportunity. If we will lead by example, proclaiming the key to living a life pleasing to the Lord, He will carry us along in *the tides of life.*

Acknowledgments

I'm grateful for the many people who have contributed to the thoughts and experiences of my life that are discussed in this book. These include my parents, my wife, Judy, my children, my grandchildren, those I have worked with, and those who have invested in me as mentors. During the writing of this book, I have also felt the touch of God's hand as I've dealt with some difficult subjects.

I am thankful for the faithful work of my assistant, Jane McGuffey, who did all the transcribing and typing of the original manuscript.

I am also very grateful for the work of Mike Hamel during the early editing of the book and the help from Lane Dennis and his team at Crossway for their guidance and careful review to bring the book to its publishable form.

And there is a special thank-you to my friend and colleague Dave Baseler for all his guidance, help, and encouragement, as he was with me from the beginning to the finish line.

Introduction

All the world's a stage,
And all the men and women merely players;
They have their exits and their entrances.

WILLIAM SHAKESPEARE

Two weeks had passed since the biopsies had been taken. I was now at my doctor's office, awaiting the results. Would he tell me I had cancer and, if so, what would that mean? Would the disease limit how long I might live?

The doctor called me into his private office and said he had some bad news and some good news. The bad news was that the tests had found cancer. The good news was that I had several treatment options, including various methods of radiation therapy and two types of surgery. As we discussed the options, it became clear to me that the more extensive surgery provided the best chance for a cancer-free result.

Although I had passed my seventieth birthday and my faith provided a firm hope for life after death, *this life* and all it included—family, friends, and the ministry of work still to be done—became my primary focus as a decision had to be made. I went through with the surgery, and I am thankful that it was successful.

This experience provided the nudge to write this book about the lessons and choices of life—lessons and choices that involve *much more* than just a stage where players make entrances and exits.

Life comes with a treasure chest of opportunities: learning and knowing yourself; developing friendships; being productive in the use of your skills and talents; leading and serving; investing yourself in the lives of others; choosing and loving a life partner; and experiencing the joy of family.

But life also has a bucketful of trials and disappointments: feeling the pain of failure; experiencing the rejection of friends or family members; grieving over the loss of loved ones; being burdened and disadvantaged by the selfish actions or incompetence of those in authority; and facing death with a terminal illness.

We have the freedom to make choices about the way we live, but we are not always in control of the circumstances or decisions that may limit the scope or quality of those choices. We did not determine the time, place, or family of our birth, or our genetics, race, or gender. As individuals, we have little or no control over the macro forces or trends affecting the growth or lack thereof of our economy. Neither do we control the major decisions and actions of the government that has authority over us. Sometimes we may feel like bystanders as the parade of life appears to move beyond our reach or active involvement.

So what is this life all about? What is the purpose and meaning of our lives and of our work? Who are we? Where do we come from? Where are we going? Do we have an existence beyond this life? What does it mean to be human? To be a person?

I believe to be human is to be unique—more than just a creature of nature. Every person has his or her own dignity, worth, and fingerprint of potential. We have the ability to determine right from wrong, to do good or evil, to love or to hate, and to invent and innovate or destroy and dissipate.

There is a spiritual side of our humanity, a dimension that calls for the development of character and a conscience that encourages us to respond to the needs of others. This spiritual side raises the question of God and whether we are created beings with eternal existence. We have choices to make about how to respond to this spiritual side of our humanity that are in our control and will determine who we are becoming and where we are going.

I am a person of faith. I have embraced the redemptive love of God, I am a follower of Jesus Christ, and I seek to learn from the example of His life. My faith is the substance of things hoped for and the reality of things not seen. It also provides confidence as I seek to understand a purpose and framework for life and have a certainty about where I am going when this life is over.

The lessons and choices discussed in this book reflect my life experiences. They include lessons that involved both good and bad choices, successes and failures, and learning to serve as I lead.

Many of the lessons involved people who cared enough for me to invest in my growth and development. The chorus of participants in my life begins with my parents, Charlie and Ruth. It includes my wife, Judy, my partner and soul mate for more than fifty-five years; her family; our four children, their spouses, and our fifteen grandchildren; and my two sisters and their families. It also includes some names you may recognize: Peter Drucker, Billy Graham, and Warren Buffett. There were many others, including partners and associates in the practice of law; college presidents, administrators, and faculty members; associates, mentors, and partners in the world of business; and colleagues and fellow board members who served with me on various governing and advisory boards.

Each played a role in this story of lessons and choices of life. At times, they served as advisers, mentors, and encouragers. At other times, they were challengers, critical observers, and opponents. There were times when they may not have realized the significance of their involvement or example, and other times when they may have been frustrated by my responses or lack thereof.

This book covers a time frame starting with my years as a troubled and rebellious teenager; spanning my life and work experiences as a husband and father, lawyer, college administrator and faculty member, and leader and CEO of a fast-growing Fortune

500 company (ServiceMaster); and concluding in a period when titles and the trappings of office were gone and the opportunities to serve and contribute multiplied.

Life is often better understood looking backward than forward. My age provides this opportunity. I trust that my story will be helpful to you as you make those choices of life that will shape who you are becoming and where you are going.

> There is a tide in the affairs of men,
> Which taken at the flood, leads to fortune;
> Omitted, all the voyage of their life
> Is bound in shallows and in miseries.
>
> WILLIAM SHAKESPEARE

1

A Framework for the Choices of Life

The winds and currents of life create
opportunities for meaningful direction—
provided there is a firm hand on the tiller

My father was a good teacher, and I loved and admired him. He taught me many lessons of life. One of those lessons involved how to sail a boat. Ever since those early days, sailing has been a part of my life and the life of my family. Most of my sailing has been on Lake Michigan and Lake Geneva in Wisconsin. However, there have also been some special times of ocean sailing, including a trip from Bar Harbor to Kennebunkport, Maine, with my cousin Jack and my two sons, and a trip among the San Juan Islands in Washington State with a good friend.

Ocean sailing requires sensitivity to the tides, the resulting currents, the changing sea levels between high and low tides, and whether you are in a period of "spring tides" or "neap tides." The tides are determined by the combined gravitational forces exerted by the moon and the sun, as well as by the rotation of the earth. These are forces that one experiences but does not see or control.

For the sailor who is leaving a harbor and steering for open water, setting out at high tide taken at the flood provides the opportunity to sail out to sea with the current, not against it. But the sailor also needs some wind to fill the sails—another force that he experiences but does not see or control. A luff in the sails—that is, a flapping of the sails in the wind—is not a sound of confusion but of hope and opportunity. All that is needed is for the sailor to trim the sails and, with a firm hand on the tiller, set a course.

A dad who took the time to invest himself
in me and whose life of faith reflected
that God's hand was on the tiller.

I have found there are tides and winds in life resulting in forces and currents that we cannot always see or control. Yet, at times, these forces create opportunities to make choices about a direction for life.

Sailing does not require unique skills, but there is a framework of learning and understanding that provides a guide for the choices required to move the boat in a desired direction. There are variables with every sailing experience. Judgments have to be made about setting a course and determining how much sail to use. During the journey, you change course from time to time, trimming and resetting your sails. All of this is part of making the most effective use of those forces of nature that you may feel but cannot see or control.

What about those choices of life—choices that must deal with the changing tides and winds of life? They, too, may involve setting a course with a purposeful destination and being flexible enough to make the needed changes. They often involve judgment and, at times, the assumption of risk, with the chance of failure. They may also involve choosing a safe harbor when the tides and winds of life are so strong and unpredictable that you can no longer navigate. Is there a framework of learning and understanding that provides a guide for making these choices?

To Own or Be Owned

As you think about a framework for life, reflect on the message of the following poem written by a friend and describing the life journey of two men:

Midnight Games

By Gordon MacDonald

Last night at a late hour,
two men, unknown to each other,
sat brooding over fifty-five years of life.
There are those moments
when the proper ingredients of mood—
time, silence, fatigue, accomplishment
and failure—
cause minds to gaze
across the sweep of existence,
playing a strange and ruthless game called
"What's it all about?"
Such ingredients being at the critical stage

The Tides of Life

forced my two acquaintances
so to begin play.

One man sat at his desk
amongst paneled royalty
in his private den
surrounded by quadraphonic noise.
In such opulence, he thought.

The other rested calloused hands
on a scratched kitchen table.
No sound afoot except
for the deep breathing of sleeping children
in the next room
and a humming wife,
preparing for bed.

"Tally the card,"
that part of man's being
that searches for accomplishment
said.
"Count the score," it cried; "make a report,
you two men,
separated by railroad tracks,
square footage, horsepower, and clout."
And so the first of the two began.

"For openers, I own a home," he said,
"with three garages, each filled with imported cars.
(I might as well say it,)
the spread is lavish,
    nothing spared to make it the best
    all around.
I own it all; it's paid for.
You could say that it's an estate.

"I own a business, and
I own three hundred persons who work for me.

(I might as well own them.)
I tell them when they must come to work;
I tell them when to eat,
how much they'll earn,
how hard they'll strive.
They call me "Mr."; some call me "Sir."
Yes, you could say that I own them.

"I own a wife
(I might as well say it).
I've capped her teeth,
imported Paris' finest,
paid for weight reduction,
exercise lessons, club memberships.
I've purchased her cosmetic beauty.
Yes, you could say that I own her.

"I own my kids
(I might as well say it).
I've paid for the college,
the car, the orthodontist,
their doctor.
I've set them in motion
with trust funds,
European vacations,
and front-page weddings.
Yes, you could say that I own them.

"I own my investments:
my property, my stocks,
my directorships
(I might as well say it).
I own my broker, too.
Without me, he'd go
from broker to broke.
Yes, you could say that I've got
everything I own under control.

"I own a reputation;
some say hard-nosed, others shrewd
(I might as well say it).
I am respected, if not loved.
    But I never started out to be loved;
    rather, that men might tremble
    at my word and decision.
I have my reputation;
yes, you could say that.

"I guess I own just about everything.
Why, then, am I so empty of spirit
    as I play this midnight game?
Why do I sit here
    wondering:
    why my wife is not here,
    why my children chose other things to do,
    if my company will survive,
    if my reputation is secure,
    if anyone likes me?
Why must I wonder
    when I own it all?"

Second half of match;
please leave that impressive scene,
cross the tracks,
count the score,
tally the card
of a second man
who plays the game.

"My house is old, my car rusting out,
    and I wonder," he thinks,
    "if the furnace will last the winter.
But (I might as well admit it)
this place owns me.
    It calls me to itself each evening

as I walk three blocks
    from the bus stop.
It beckons with memories
    of Christmases, crisis,
      giggles, and prayers.
I am gladly owned by its warmth.

"My job . . . is a job, humbling;
    its income modest.
But (I might as well admit it)
it kind of owns me—
    its opportunities to serve others,
    to fix things,
    make them go and click,
    to make something
    with these hands of mine,
    some sense of accomplishment,
    producing finished things from raw.
You could say I like what I'm doing.

"My wife, listen to her hum off key,
    was not a cheerleader,
    and Wellesley is not her background.
But (I might as well admit it)
    she owns me; I belong to her.
    So compelling her affection,
    so deep her insight,
    so broad her perspective,
    so eternal her values,
    so compassionate her caring.
I gladly give myself to her.
You could say that I am possessed,
nothing held back.

"My children; hear them toss in troubled sleep,
    average students,
    reasonable competitors.

They (I might as well be frank about it)
  own me.
I cannot withhold my time from them,
  my unrestrained enjoyment as
  they discover life and allow me
  to join them as both
  player and spectator.
The birth certificates say they are mine.
  But my heart says they own me.

"As to my assets,
  I own nothing Wall Street admires
(I might as well admit it).
  A few things perhaps,
  but largely unredeemable.
All my holdings are in love,
  in friendship,
  in memories and discoveries
  about life.
You could say that I am glad to be alive,
  even if
  my estate
  is pure sentimentality.

"Reputation?
  No man knows me or fears me,
  unless you count my friends.
And (I might as well lay it on the table)
  they own me.
  Why, I'd jump to their side
  should occasion arise.
  I'd laugh,
  I'd cry,
  I'd give,
  I'd die,
  I'd hold nothing back from them.

You could say my friends own me;
I have no regrets."

Tally the card; count the score,
the souls of two men cry out.
One owns, the other is owned.
> Who is winner?
> Are you as confused as I,
> as we watch two men
> extinguish the lights
> and go to bed?
> One face is smiling
> and humming off key.
> The other is frightened,
> listening to silence.

Perhaps we counted wrongly?
Perhaps we didn't know soon enough,
> it was a different game
> with different rules
> and a different judge,
> mounting to different and
> very high stakes.

What will be your reflections on the journey of your life ten, twenty, or thirty years from now? As you think about this poignant story, don't get lost in the fact that one man had a lot of money and the other did not. The issue goes deeper than money, wealth, and riches. It speaks to those fundamental choices of life that can be made only on an individual basis. Will those choices be made within a framework of life with you at the center and with a focus on what you want and what you think you own and control, or one that is more other-oriented and includes the role of God in your life—Someone you cannot see but Whom you can trust with the ownership of who you are and who you are becoming?

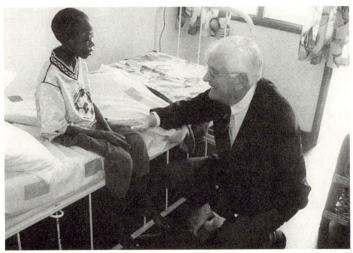

The opportunities to serve are many as one seeks to be owned.

Out of Africa

As you consider what it means to own or be owned, let me take you to Africa to meet people making life choices in cultures and environments very different from what we in the Western world normally know and experience.

Several years ago, I went to Kenya and Uganda with a representative from Opportunity International to visit some of that organization's microfinance banks. The trip also involved a separate visit to northern Uganda and southern Sudan with representatives from Samaritan's Purse to visit some of its relief and medical work.

As I listened to a bank manager explaining how the bank had been established and how small loans, ranging from $150 to $300 per person, were providing opportunities for the poor, I was amazed and overwhelmed by the results that were being achieved. But only when I got out into the villages and heard from the clients did I realize the true significance of what was being accomplished in the lives of people.

It went far beyond financial transactions involving loans and repayment with interest. Through Opportunity International's trust bank concept, it also touched questions involving the purpose and meaning of life, the importance of relationships, and the dignity and worth of each borrower. It was all about fulfilling the organization's mission of "giving the working poor a chance."

I still remember the day I was with a group of women clients in a small village hut with a dirt floor, listening to stories about their businesses and their loans. When I asked why they needed to borrow more money, one woman spoke up on behalf of the group. She said that although each of them had separate businesses, they were all involved in a common project. Each had taken into her family several children who were orphans because their parents had died of AIDS. She went on to explain that there were still more orphans in the village who were without loving care. The women needed loans so they could grow their businesses and have additional income to support the costs of taking in these children to be part of their families.

In our Western way of thinking, we might have initially classified these women as poor, using only an economic scale as the basis for our conclusion. But they did not think of themselves as poor. They were not poor in spirit. They were rich in their choices to be other-oriented. Where did the spark for this type of choice come from? Did it have anything to do with their framework for life, a framework that was guided by their faith in God? My subsequent conversations with them confirmed that it did.

The next leg of my trip was a flight in a single-prop plane to northern Uganda with friends from Samaritan's Purse. We visited refugee camps where Samaritan's Purse was providing food and shelter. The refugees had been displaced by a group of bandits who called themselves the "Lord's Resistance Army." These bandits not only took away their homes, possessions, and lands, but also stole their children, turning the boys into soldiers and the girls into sex slaves. The refugee camp was filled with broken people seeking to survive with their broken families. It was a stark reminder of the anguish and pain caused by a few evil people who chose power and control for themselves at the expense of many. What is it about the nature of our humanity that feeds such a choice of evil over good?

We then flew over hills and mountains to a mission hospital in southern Sudan. The hospital had recently been bombed by the government of northern Sudan in the ongoing civil war with roots in the religious differences between Islam (predominant in the north) and Christianity (predominant in the south). The bombs had fallen several days before, and while it had been a close call, fortunately the hospital had not been hit and no one had been injured.

As we approached what should have been a small airstrip, there was nothing but a field of grass ten feet high. The pilot circled the area several times and saw what he thought was a good place to land. It was a most interesting landing. Soon, a truck came through the tall grass to take us where we were scheduled to visit. Along the way, we passed through a small village. All the people were waving a welcome to us.

As we approached the hospital, we had to drive between two craters caused by the recent bombing. The hospital and the patient waiting rooms in some of the outer buildings were teeming with people receiving care and waiting for care.

We were greeted by a young physician from America and two young nurses, one from America and one from Canada. They had just finished a skin graft on a young boy who had fallen into a cooking fire the day before.

They gave us a tour and told us the history of the hospital, which at one time had been at the center of a thriving mission compound. The doctor shared about the variety of health problems they could treat. All three were excited about their work and were very grateful for the medicines, supplies, a new generator, and other equipment Samaritan's Purse had provided.

By the time we finished the tour, it was late afternoon. We sat down for a cup of tea outside their sleeping tents. It was 110 degrees and they were looking forward to nightfall, when it would cool down to 100 degrees. Their typical evening involved some reading by lantern light, then getting some rest so they would be prepared for the duties of the next day.

When I inquired about what motivated them to choose such a difficult and dangerous place to serve, they referred to their faith and described their work as a calling from God to use their medical skills, talents, and the strength and energy of their relatively young ages to serve in a difficult environment where there was a critical need.

The man in the poem who was "owned," the women in Uganda, and the young professionals in Sudan all had a framework for their choices of life that involved God and reflected a passionate and high view of the dignity and worth of every person. Such a view was absent in the framework of life held by the other man in the poem, who focused on himself and what he thought he owned. The same could be said of the leaders of the "Lord's Resistance Army" in northern Uganda, who were consumed by choices for power and control over others, or of those in northern Sudan who determined that the use of bombs as agents of destruction and death would further their religious and political purposes.

To Be Responsible and Free

So what is our humanity all about? Do we simply represent the highest form of animal life in the evolutionary chain or is there something more; something unique about who we are, such as our desire to be free, our ability to know and do good or evil, and our fingerprint of potential as created beings?

One response to these questions is found in the Declaration of Independence of the United States. In the opening words, it declares it is a self-evident truth that God created us equal and endowed us with "certain unalienable rights." This conviction was central to the signers' declaration of their right to be free from the restraints and taxation of a government that did not provide equality of representation.

As humans, we have a natural desire to be free and to choose how we live. However, legitimate restraints may be imposed on our freedom for the common good. We are also accountable for the consequences of our choices. Freedom without responsibility is anarchy.

Human history records many abuses and unreasonable restraints of freedom. To help our children understand some of this history, Judy and I took them to Europe for a "freedom appreciation tour" at a time when our older children were in college and our younger children were in high school.

One of our stops was Berlin. At that time, it was still a divided city. It still had that vivid symbol of man's attempt to extinguish freedom, the Berlin Wall. This massive concrete structure split and segregated the great city. The wall spoke of a mind-set that feared freedom and trusted in man-made barriers. These barriers were constructed not only to contain those within but to bar those from without. Yet no matter how formidable the obstacle, there continued to be regular escapes to the West as people risked their lives for liberty.

A visit to East Berlin through Checkpoint Charlie included a forced purchase of twenty-five East German marks per person and an opportunity to shop at stores with little or no merchandise. We experienced a feeling of confinement and constraint as we saw uniformed "peace" guards on every block and witnessed a façade of artificial uniformity in the drab dress of the people and the plain cars in the street.

Our next stop was the Dachau concentration camp. During the 1930s, people in Germany forfeited their freedom by supporting the tyrannical Nazi government of Adolf Hitler. Our visit to this infamous camp reminded us of the depths of human evil and the great deception of corrupt power. The first thing a prisoner saw as he entered the camp was the sign above the gate: "*Arbeit Macht Frei*" ("Work Makes One Free"), an evil lie to all who passed through. Within two hundred yards of the gate, behind another wall, were the gas chambers and crematoriums that became the final destination of thousands of Jews and others.

Beyond these prison walls and several hundred miles away, we visited a beautiful fairyland castle in the Bavarian hills. It was the vision of a madman who just happened to be the king of Bavaria. For forty years, his every wish was everyone else's command. He conscripted the men of Bavaria to build his castle. They were forced to work so the king's dreams could be fulfilled. Ironically, he was able to use the completed castle only for six months before he died a mysterious death. Yes, he had freedom—he could choose anything he wanted—but only on the backs of those he ruled. And at his death, he, like everyone else, had no choice but to leave his dream behind.

The luxury of choice for a few at the expense of many is tyranny, not freedom. When death comes, freedom of choice for this life is gone. Freedom should not be used as a license to simply please or amuse oneself.

Leaving Germany, we went on to Amsterdam, a city with a reputation as one of the freest cities in the world—so free that narcotics were legally sold and used in the streets, prostitution was open and legal, and a once-beautiful city park had become the permanent love-in dormitory for young people from all over the world. As we walked the streets, our children were overwhelmed by the beauty of the city, but also with the sadness of seeing the results of freedom abused. Freedom carries responsibility with it. Abused freedom can become a vehicle of self-destruction as people focus solely on themselves and their personal pleasure.

Sometimes sacrifice is required if freedom is to be preserved. Our last stop was a cemetery in Holland where we saw row upon row of white crosses representing the final resting places of young Americans who gave their lives on foreign soil to preserve our right to be free. It was an especially poignant time for my eighteen-year-old son, who identified the grave of a soldier his own age.

This trip had a profound influence on our children. It provided a living reminder of the value of the freedom they enjoyed as Americans and the responsibility they had as they made choices to exercise that freedom in ways consistent with their faith.

To Know Right and Do What I Ought

There is more to being human than our common desire to be free. There is a moral or spiritual dimension to our humanity. It is often described as a function of our brains called the conscience. It accounts for our sense of what we "ought" to do. When we fail to do what we "ought" or do something we "ought not," we experience a sense of guilt or shame.

C. S. Lewis, the celebrated Oxford don and author, suggested that this dimension of our humanity reflects God working within us to influence or command us to behave in a certain way. In his book *Mere Christianity*, he described it this way: "Something which . . . appears in me as a law urging me to do right and making me feel responsible and uncomfortable when I do wrong." Lewis further said that the working of this moral law is common to all humanity and reflects the greatness of God as our Creator. In his book *The Problem of Pain*, he wrote, "All the human beings that history has heard of acknowledge some kind of morality; that is, they feel towards certain proposed actions the experiences expressed by the words 'I ought' or 'I ought not.'"

Lewis also recognized that as humans we can nurture and respond to these moral influences or suppress and resist them. He concluded by saying, "Virtue . . . brings light; indulgence brings fog."

Lewis's views about the moral dimension of our humanity and the reality of God the Creator are discussed in detail in *The Question of God* by Dr. Armand Nicholi. In this book, Nicholi compares Lewis's life and worldview with those of Sigmund Freud. When he wrote the book, Nicholi was a practicing psychiatrist and a professor at the Harvard Medical School and Harvard College. The book was an outgrowth of a class he taught at both schools on the lives and views of Lewis and Freud. I have known Armand as a friend. His life and the way he was able to affirm but not impose his faith in his teaching and relationships with his students have been an inspiration and example to me.

Both Lewis and Freud made significant contributions to the development of their respective disciplines. Both started their professional careers as atheists. Lewis became a Christian, but Freud died an atheist. Freud's life and views have contributed significantly to the growing secularization in Western society. On the other hand, Lewis's writings have become a primary voice in proclaiming the reality of God and the importance of developing a relationship with Him through the redemptive work of His Son, Jesus Christ. Although each man gave a different answer, both agreed that the most important question in life was the question of the existence of God. How people answer this question determines the framework for their choices of life.

To Know God and Be Known by Him

The complexity and design of human nature point to God as our Creator. The reality of our freedom, our ability to do good or evil, and the presence of a moral conscience confirm a spiritual dimension to our humanity, with God as the ultimate source of truth and moral authority.

These ideas are not new, and they should not be pigeonholed as simply personal or religious views discussed only among those of a common belief. I realize that in an increasingly secular society, such views are often so categorized in an attempt to be tolerant or to be politically correct. But when we do so, we seek to hide the possibility of a truth that may reflect an authority above and beyond ourselves; an authority to which we are and will be accountable for the choices we make in life.

When my son Chip was in Harvard Law School, he sent me a letter expressing his frustration and concern about the way Roe vs. Wade, the 1973 Supreme Court case that determined that women have the constitutional right to abort their babies, was discussed in his constitutional law class. He said there seemed to be no interest in talking about the moral issues in the case because the professor and a majority of the students had already concluded there was no way to determine or reach a consensus as to what was morally correct. The desire to be tolerant short-circuited a meaningful time of learning and discussion regarding how to understand a legal system that could determine murder is wrong and subject to the death penalty but abortion is legal and protected by the Constitution. Is there no longer room to raise the question of God and His standards when we have a public discussion of the extent to which we as a society should value and protect the sanctity of life?

In addition to Lewis, a chorus of respected thought leaders from various walks of life would reject such an exclusion. They have embraced the existence of God and His role as our Creator. They have explored the wonder and uniqueness of our humanity, including its spiritual dimension, as part of developing a framework of life—a worldview or value system—that is not relative and that recognizes God as the ultimate authority.

For instance, Alexander Solzhenitsyn, in his classic work *The Gulag Archipelago*, recognized that a line between good and evil passes though every human heart. He suggested that even in hearts overwhelmed by evil, there is one small bridgehead of good, and even in the best of hearts, there remains a small corner of evil. He concluded that it is impossible to expel evil from the world in its entirety, but it is possible to recognize it and restrain it. For Solzhenitsyn, the ultimate source of good and restraint of evil is God the Creator, an authority beyond all men.

In his 1978 Harvard University commencement address entitled *A World Split Apart*, Solzhenitsyn framed the issue as follows:

> I am not examining the case of a disaster brought on by a world war and the changes which it would produce in society. . . . I am referring to the calamity of an autonomous, irreligious, humanistic consciousness. . . .
>
> Is it true that man is above everything? Is there no Superior Spirit [God] above him? Is it right that man's life and society's activities should be ruled by a material expansion above all? Is it permissible to promote such expansion to the detriment of our integral spiritual life?
>
> If the world has not approached its end, it has reached a major watershed in history, equal in importance to the turn from the Middle Ages to the Renaissance. It will demand from us a spiritual blaze; we shall have to rise to a new height of vision, to a new level of life, where our physical nature will not be cursed, as in the Middle Ages, but even more importantly, our spiritual being will not be trampled upon, as in the Modern Era.

These words came from a man who grew up and was trained in a system that rejected the existence of God. He had embraced the Marxist philosophy that humanity and the material world were the ultimate reality and that God was dead. Humans had all the answers and set their own standards. Religion was an illusion, reality was rooted in material well-being, and socialism was inevitable. Something happened to Solzhenitsyn, however, that dramatically changed his view of life.

After serving as a captain in the Red Army, Solzhenitsyn was arrested under Josef Stalin's reign of terror and forced to live in the horror of Soviet prison camps for many years. As he later described in detail in *The Gulag Archipelago*, in prison he found a higher purpose in life. There is something more to life than just an entrance and an exit. Through the testimony of fellow prisoners and the prison doctor, who had converted from Judaism to Christianity, Solzhenitsyn found God, committed his life to Him, and became a follower of Jesus Christ. Little did he realize that he would later receive a Nobel Prize for Literature or that he would eventually be released to live in the freedom of the West. In a published interview, he described the experience of finding his starting point with God as follows: "The 'ideology [of Communism] disappears completely' and is stripped bare by camp life; 'first comes the fight for survival, then discovery of life, then God.'"

A short time before Solzhenitsyn was arrested in the Soviet Union, Dietrich Bonhoeffer came to the end of his physical life in Germany. He was a prisoner of another godless system, the Third Reich. Bonhoeffer was a pastor and a theologian. He believed in acting on his faith and resisting a system of evil that rejected God as Creator. During the 1930s, he was a minority voice speaking out against the evils of Nazism, a philosophy that espoused the superiority of one race over another. No man, he declared, not even Hitler, is superior to God, and every person has been created in God's image with dignity and worth. In the 1940s, Bonhoeffer was arrested, and during his extended prison stay he wrote several essays and letters dealing with the meaning and purpose of life. Reflect upon this quote from a letter written just months before he was executed by the Gestapo:

Who stands fast? Only the man whose final standard is not his reason, his principles, his conscience, his freedom, or his virtue, but who is ready to sacrifice all this when he is called to obedient and responsible action in faith and in exclusive allegiance to God—the responsible man, who tries to make his whole life an answer to the question and call of God. Where are these responsible people?

Both Solzhenitsyn and Bonhoeffer experienced the evils of a godless system. They saw the depths of man's inhumanity to man. Yet, through it all, their faith in God remained and was affirmed. Both men said in their own way that the question of God cannot be ignored. It is inherent in the spiritual dimension of our humanity, and when there are attempts to suppress it, trivialize it, or block it out, evil has the opportunity to flourish.

Integration of Faith and Work

Another thought leader who recognized the importance of understanding the value of our humanity, including its spiritual dimension, was Peter Drucker. Drucker is often referred to as the father of modern-day management. During my years of leadership at ServiceMaster, he was an adviser, mentor, and friend, and I learned much from him.

In 1989, I was asked to speak at his eightieth birthday celebration. My assignment was to speak about the characteristics needed for the effective executive of the 1990s. The task seemed larger than life, especially in view of the distinguished audience and my respect for Peter's wisdom. In my talk, I emphasized the importance of leaders knowing what they believed and why they believed it, and being willing to serve the people they lead while assuming responsibility for their development as a whole person, not just as pairs of hands.

This theme was similar to one Peter had addressed two years earlier when accepting the honor of having the Management School at Claremont Graduate University named after him:

> Management is, by itself, a liberal art. It has to be. . . . It cannot be concerned solely with results and performance. Precisely because the object of management is a human community held

together for a common purpose by the work bond, management always deals with the nature of man and woman—and by the way, as all of us with any practical experience learned, with the nature of God and, alas, "with [the nature of evil]." . . . That means that there have to be values, commitment, convictions in management, yes, even passion. Without them, there will be no performance and no results. Indeed, since management deals with people and not with things, management without values, commitments, [and] convictions can only do harm. . . . St. Bonaventure said, "All knowledge leads back to the Source of All Light and to the knowledge of ultimate truth." . . . The spirit of St. Bonaventure's short sentence must animate all we do if management is to have results.

In a recent book entitled *Drucker's Lost Art of Management,* Joe Maciariello, the world's leading Drucker scholar, and his colleague Karen Linkletter explore this theme that the management of people is a liberal art. Their book reflects extensive scholarly research into Drucker's philosophy of life and spiritual worldview, and confirms the discussions I had with Peter on these subjects.

The authors note that while Drucker was private about his faith, he often referred to himself as a very conventional and traditional Christian. For Drucker, faith brought a personal meaning and purpose to life. On questions of faith and the nature of our humanity, he was profoundly influenced by the writings of Søren Kierkegaard, the Dutch philosopher and theologian of the nineteenth century. In his essay "The Unfashionable Kierkegaard," Drucker wrote:

Human existence is possible as existence not in despair, as existence not in tragedy; it is possible as existence in faith. . . . Faith is the belief that in God the impossible is possible, that in Him time and eternity are one, that both life and death are meaningful. Faith is the knowledge that man is a creature—not autonomous, not the master, not the end, not the center—and yet responsible and free.

Drucker took an interest in the ServiceMaster business model because he saw us implementing his view of management as a liberal art as we sought to affirm the role of faith without imposing it while doing business. He saw ServiceMaster as not only an example of a successful business, but also as a moral community committed to the development of human character.

I witnessed the integration of faith and work at ServiceMaster firsthand. For twenty-five years, I had the privilege to participate in the leadership of the company and to inherit and build on the objectives and culture that my three predecessors had established.

Marion Wade, ServiceMaster's founder, had the vision not only to start and grow a successful service business, but also to bring his faith out of the pew on Sunday to his work on Monday. He believed his faith should influence how he conducted his business and treated the people working with him. As the business grew, Marion recruited a pastor, Ken Hansen, as a partner in the business. Ken had a keen mind and the ability to think strategically. He soon recognized, however, that his training in theology was not sufficient for the task, and he secured his MBA at the University of Chicago.

As the business continued to grow, Ken recruited Ken Wessner to join the company. Wes had great sales and operational skills, and could always see both the forest and the trees. He made many contributions to the growth of our business, including establishing and providing leadership for our health care management services business.

Although different in personalities, skills, and talents, these three leaders had a framework for their choices of life that included a commitment to integrate the claims of their Christian faith with the demands of their work.

By the time I joined ServiceMaster in 1977, Marion had passed away, Ken was chairman, and Wes was CEO. Ken and Wes became my tutors and mentors. I learned from them and many others what it meant to bring my faith to the doing of business and to embrace the objectives of the firm: "To Honor God in All We Do; To Help People Develop; To Pursue Excellence; and To Grow Profitably."

My Faith Journey

When it comes to the development of my framework for the choices I have made in life, nothing has been as formative as my journey of faith.

To begin with, I am thankful for the heritage of Christian parents. They were faithful followers of Jesus Christ in both word and deed.

A mother who embraced the reality of her faith and led me to mine.

During my grade-school years, there came a time when I realized there was a choice to be made whether I wanted to become a follower of Christ. My mother helped me understand the significance of the choice before me by sharing passages from the Bible that pointed out the reality of sin, the need for forgiveness if I were to have a relationship with God, and God's offer of love and forgiveness through the redemptive work of His Son, Jesus Christ. She emphasized that God wanted a relationship with me, but first I had to choose to accept His offer. It was a choice that only I could make, and to do so I had to put my faith and trust in a God I could not see. Once made, she said, the choice would be a completed transaction with God and I would begin the process of learning to know Him and be known by Him.

Although young and unsophisticated, I was able to make that choice. I took the step of commitment and faith, turned to God, and accepted His gift for me. Some use the biblical term "born again" to refer to this point of commitment. It was the beginning of my learning what it would mean to be a follower of Jesus Christ.

This relationship with Christ is available to all, but like any offer, it cannot become a completed transaction unless there is a choice of acceptance, faith, and commitment. When this choice is made, there is a hope not only for this life but for an eternal life with God. It is a decision that goes beyond the fast pace of this world, with all its challenges and uncertainties, successes and failures, and involves the understanding that life is an ongoing process of becoming all that God wants us to be.

Because the Christian life results in a growing relationship with God, it has provided me a framework for making choices leading to a life worth living. This life includes learning and seeking *to be owned and other-oriented; to be responsible in the exercise of my freedom; to know right, avoid wrong, and do what I ought; and to know God and be known by Him.* There have been failures, mistakes, and poor choices along the way, but God has used them to teach me about repentance, forgiveness, and His faithful love.

In addition to my relationship with God, the most important relationships in my life have been with my wife and my family.

45

A partnership for life that resulted in the joy of family.

Judy and I were high school sweethearts. We made the choice to wed at the end of our junior year in college. We have now been married for more than fifty-five years. It is God's standard and His way that I love and cherish my wife. I am not the superior; she is not the subordinate. It's not my checkbook, my house, my way. We have become a partnership based on mutual love and trust and our common faith in God. Judy and I are committed to each other and continue to work at the joining of our separate and distinct personalities. This requires constant attention to smoothing the rough edges.

The most important results of this partnership are the four children God has given us. Our role has been to provide unconditional love and a home for their development, admonition, and spiritual nurture. Though each child is different and our role has changed as they matured, we have a continuing responsibility to guide their development and to love and accept their chosen life partners. We also have a role in the guidance of our fifteen grandchildren. They are all God's children as well as ours.

Yes, for me there have been times of doubt and despair, especially through some difficult teenage years and the sudden death of my father when I was eighteen. There followed the challenges of college and law school, of establishing a home, supporting a family, and financing an education. There were also times when there were failures, mistakes, feelings of inadequacy, and concerns about whether I would measure up.

Finally, I have experienced wonderful relationships in my work life. After college, I practiced law for ten years, then made a dramatic change when I went to Wheaton College to serve as an administrator and faculty member. Then, in the fall of 1977, my career took another turn when I joined the leadership team at ServiceMaster. I spent the years that followed seeking to learn, lead, and serve in a fast-growing public company. In so doing, I came to understand the great benefits of working with and learning from others who shared the common goal of seeking to honor God in all they did and who made their lives a witness and example of the God they loved.

Many of the chapters that follow deal with issues I have faced in seeking to integrate my faith with my work, especially the work of business. It has become a calling and the primary ministry of my life.

The Tides of Life

Robert Louis Stevenson once said that when God came into his life, "I came about like a well-handled ship." As a sailor, I know what it means to come about. It results in a change of course. In a strong wind, such a change of course requires a steady hand on the tiller. My life has involved "coming about" on several occasions, including career decisions. As I look back, I can see that these changes were all part of a framework of life that involved sailing with God and allowing His hand to be on the tiller. To know Him is to be known by Him.

> The steadfast love of the LORD never ceases,
> his mercies never come to an end;
> they are new every morning;
> great is your faithfulness.
> "The LORD is my portion," says my soul,
> "therefore I will hope in Him."
> (Lamentations 3:22–24, NRSV)

2

The Persistent Question of Fairness in an Uneven World

Judge carefully, for with the LORD our God there is no injustice.

2 CHRONICLES 19:7, NIV

Life is not always a bowl full of cherries. It is not always equal. It is not always fair. It is not always just. We live in an uneven world—uneven in the circumstances of birth, of opportunity, and of the exercise of authority. How, then, do we navigate in these sometimes treacherous waters of life where there are currents of inequality, unfairness, and injustice?

Will a framework of life determined by our faith provide a waypoint or guide for how we should respond to these uneven currents?

As I write this book, the sports headlines are about the "leap of faith" that launched a new star. Jeremy Lin, the first American-born player of Chinese or Taiwanese descent to play in the NBA, has risen from a benchwarmer to a global basketball star in just fourteen days. How did he go unnoticed for so long?

All of a sudden, Lin, a 6'3" guard with an economics degree

from Harvard and a faith in God, just happened to be the one to give the struggling New York Knicks a renewed hope that they could have a better season after all.

Education Secretary Arne Duncan, who also played at Harvard and has developed a relationship with Lin, was quoted as saying: "Everyone who thinks this is an overnight success fundamentally gets this wrong. Jeremy has been a very good player for a long time and just never had the opportunity."

How does such a thing happen in a highly competitive, well-organized professional sport like basketball? The system and incentives are in place to identify the very best players for the NBA—not only in America but in the world. As some newspaper articles suggest, there may have been some unspoken perceptions or discriminatory feelings among general managers, coaches, or scouts that a smart, clean-cut Asian American under 6'5" was just not the "type" to make it. He was a good player at Harvard, but he was not drafted by any NBA team. Before coming to the Knicks, he was picked up and then cut by the Golden State Warriors and later by the Houston Rockets.

Even with all this attention, Lin remains humble: "I want to be the same person before and after. That's where I want to be. I don't want to let anything affect me or our team."

This statement suggests something about the "person" of Jeremy Lin. It suggests he has a framework for the choices of life that reaches beyond his skills in basketball and the unfairness of the stereotyping of others; a framework that includes faith as a sustaining force, with a purpose that extends beyond the unevenness of life. When he writes his book, we will know more about the person of Jeremy Lin.

Learning to Swim in an Uneven World

During my teenage years, there were some uneven currents in my life. At times, the hand of discipline from some teachers and certain administrators caused me to be cynical and wary of those in authority. I trusted my parents and accepted their direction, but had a rebellious attitude with respect to others in authority. I had some lessons to learn.

For about eighteen months after my high school graduation, the uneven currents of life seemed overwhelming at times, but the resulting pain of adversity was a gift that helped me become more accepting of the reality of this unevenness and lean on the supportive role of my faith.

Like many young people in their senior year of high school, I wanted to go to college. Judy, my high school sweetheart, and I both had decided we wanted to go to the college in our hometown: Wheaton College in Wheaton, Illinois. The problem was that Judy's scores on the standardized college admission tests were higher than mine. She received her admission letter in the spring before graduation, while I received a letter putting me on a waiting list.

Because of the high academic standards at Wheaton and because of my relatively low test scores, my school adviser suggested I either apply to other schools or consider not going to college. But I had dreamed of playing football at Wheaton and, much to my parents' chagrin, had decided not to apply to other schools. I determined that if I didn't get into Wheaton, I wouldn't go to college at all. Instead, I would get a job in either the painting or construction business, as I had worked in both these areas during the summer months of high school.

The summer dragged on and it was mid-August before I received any word from Wheaton. The football coach (who would become one of those adult role models in my life) called and told me I had been accepted for the fall semester on a provisional basis. Whether I could continue at Wheaton would depend on my grades at the end of the first semester. He then invited me to football camp the week before school started. I received a confirming letter a few days later from the Admissions Office. I went to camp with an enthusiastic spirit, focused upon achieving success in football and in my studies.

We both made it! Registration Day as freshmen at Wheaton College.

By the third day of football camp, I began fainting during the scrimmages. The trainer first thought it might be heat exhaustion, but when it happened again the next day, they took me to the hospital and handed me over to a team of doctors. After a series of tests, they determined I had a bleeding ulcer in my duodenum. Football was out of the question for the fall semester. They would try a strict diet of soft foods for several months before they would decide whether surgery was necessary.

The cafeteria at the college wasn't suited to the requirements of my diet, so I began my freshman year not just sitting on the sidelines, but sitting in the stands with the dream of playing football gone and eating all my meals at home. As a result, I did not have the same opportunity as others to develop friendships on the team or with other students eating together in the dining hall. I spent an inordinate amount of time studying in the school library so I could qualify to continue at Wheaton. Despite my being such a bore, Judy stuck with me, although she had plenty of opportunities to date others.

By the end of the first semester, my grades were good enough to qualify as a regular student, the ulcer was healed, and I could go back on a more regular diet and eat in the dining hall.

One morning during the first week of March, I was called out of class by the assistant dean of students. He had just received news that my father had suffered a heart attack and was in a hospital in Nashville. I was to call home.

This was my father's second heart attack. I knew it must be serious. When I called home, my sister told me her husband Jim had already purchased tickets for the two of us to fly to Nashville that afternoon. By the time we arrived at the hospital, my father was in a deep sleep. As I consoled my mother, she told me the doctors had said the next twenty-four hours would be critical.

It was a long night of waiting and praying before the sun came up and my father woke from his induced sleep. When he saw me, he smiled and asked me how school was going and whether I was still thinking about the plan we had discussed for me to transfer the next fall to the engineering school at Northwestern University. I assured him the plan was still in place and that I had already sent in my application to Northwestern.

As we finished our conversation, several nurses came in and asked us to step into the hall while they did some work on my dad. After about fifteen minutes, the red light suddenly went on over the door of my father's room and the loudspeaker proclaimed: "Code Blue! Code Blue!" Several more nurses and doctors rushed into his room.

It may have been only five or ten minutes, but it seemed much longer until a doctor came out and told us my father had suffered another massive heart attack and was dead.

My immediate thoughts related to my mother and how I could help and support her now and in the days ahead. It would be a long ride home in my dad's car as Jim and I shared the driving responsibilities.

During the days that followed, which included the funeral, my mother grieved over the loss of her husband. However, for me she was a pillar of strength and reflected the peace of God and the assurance of her faith that to be absent from the body is to be present with the Lord (2 Corinthians 5:8).

My dad's death had a sobering effect on all of us. He was the leader of our family. He was wise and caring. He had always been there when we needed him. He was a faithful attendee at all my athletic events in high school. He never had the opportunity to go to college and he had been very supportive of me becoming an engineer.

My mother was only fifty-one years old when my dad died. What would her future look like? My oldest sister, Virginia, was married with two children. Jim, her husband, worked in my father's business. What would his future look like? My sister JoAnn had just been married, and her husband, Don, was in the Army. I was a freshman in college, still struggling with whether I could ever measure up to being an engineer.

Why did my father have to die now? It was unfair to all of us. Why did God take him now? We all needed him. What was it all about?

The second day after the funeral, I was back at school, walking across campus. I met the president of the college, Dr. V. Raymond Edman, who was walking the other way back to his office. I had never met him before on a personal basis, and although I had received a note from him saying that he and his wife were praying for me and my family, I did not expect him to recognize me. So I was surprised when he called me by my first name and asked me to stop and talk with him for a moment. His words were very consoling, and he concluded with a statement I will never forget: "Bill, don't doubt in the dark what you have seen in the light."

It was a great reminder to me that my faith, as described in the book of Hebrews, was "the assurance of things hoped for, the conviction of things not seen" (Hebrews 11:1, NASB). My faith provided the confidence of knowing where my father was and that someday I would see him again.

The spring semester soon passed. I had received my acceptance from Northwestern and was planning to transfer to its engineering school in the fall. For summer work, I was able to get a job with a painting contractor.

Without my father's leadership, his business was not doing well and soon declared bankruptcy. The provision he had made for my mother to receive income from the business was now gone. Her only assets were our house and a monthly check from my father's life insurance that amounted to less than $200.

She soon decided to sell our home, and my sister and brother-in-law also decided to sell their home. With their combined resources, they bought a house that would accommodate, with some limited sleeping quarters, my mother and me, as well as my sister's family. I was thankful for my summer job, because now there would be no money from my family for school tuition.

Northwestern's fall semester started in late September. As I went through the registration process, I realized for the first time that Northwestern was not going to accept credits for most of my courses at Wheaton. In the school's judgment, the liberal arts courses I had taken did not fit with an engineering degree. This meant I had wasted my year at Wheaton. I appealed the decision, but no one listened to the merits of my case. So, with some anxiety over what my father would have thought about terminating our dream of an engineering degree from Northwestern, I decided to withdraw.

My brother-in-law encouraged me to explore other alternatives, and the next week I discovered that the University of Illinois would accept me into its engineering program and would accept all my Wheaton credits. The only problem was that its fall semester had started three weeks earlier. However, the school would still accept me. I immediately enrolled in the initial required courses for an engineering degree, including calculus, physics, and chemistry, and chalked up the Northwestern experience as just another case of the uneven hand of authority.

I soon realized how far behind I was and, after attending a

month of classes, I also realized that only failure lay ahead if I were to continue. So I also withdrew from the University of Illinois. I had enough of "education" and started looking for a full-time job. By this time, my mother was starting to get anxious about my decisions and to wonder what would become of me.

My brother-in-law helped me get a job selling industrial lift trucks during the day and I got a second job at Marshall Field selling men's clothes at night. The selling experience was good for me, but I also had a growing awareness that I needed a college education. By the time Christmas was over, I had earned enough money to go back to school, and with the encouragement of my mom and Judy, I decided to go back to Wheaton. In early January, I enrolled for the spring semester as a business and economics major with a goal of catching up with my former classmates so I could graduate with them in June 1960.

Although I was careful not to show it, I was still grieving the death of my father. I had feelings of letting him down because I was not pursuing an engineering degree. As a result of what I had experienced and the choices I had made during this eighteen-month period, I had developed a fear of failure and seriously wondered whether I would measure up to his expectations. I found myself again asking God those "why" questions for which there were no ready answers. Life during this period had been painful, but there still was hope for the future. I had a little money in my pocket and I had chosen to go back to school.

The Power of Pain

Although I did not understand it at the time, God was using these painful experiences to break and mold me. The death of my father and the sorrow I felt in his absence led to my birth as a man. I had made some bad choices and I was responsible for those choices. I still had the responsibility to help in the care and support of my mother. It would now be up to me. My dad was no longer around to help her or me. I was learning about the consequences of my choices in life. I was learning about my responsibility for others. I was experiencing the pain of growth as part of my preparation for the future. That pain confirmed the reality that, no matter what had occurred in the past, there would be opportunities in the future. Pain was a message of life.

Years later, when I was going through some painful experiences in business, I learned of a powerful example of this principle. It involved a man who had the practice of once a month dipping his entire body in scalding hot water so that he could feel the sensation of pain in every extremity of his body. This man was Dr. Paul Brand, a medical missionary who was in charge of a large leprosarium at a remote mission station. The only way he could effectively test whether he had contracted the dreaded disease of leprosy was to feel the sensation of pain. Pain meant life. As he felt the pain over his entire body, including the tips of his fingers and tips of his toes, he knew there was life and he had not contracted the disease.

For me, the pain during this period was more mental than physical and came with the disappointment of rejection, failure, the loss of my father, the anxiety of taking the risk of the unknown, and the challenge of stretching to reach that next accomplishment or objective.

As a Christian, I have come to believe that, as part of experiencing pain in this life, God has called us to share His pain and to learn that life begins with dying to self and freedom comes from surrendering to His way. God reminds us in Psalm 46:1 that He "is our refuge and strength, a very present help in trouble," and in 2 Corinthians 4:17 that "our light and momentary troubles are achieving for us an eternal glory that far outweighs them all" (NIV).

In God's plan, our pain is often the crucible for understanding His love. But God's goodness and love are different from many of the popular understandings of these words. They cannot be equated with achieving a state of happiness in which it doesn't matter what we do as long as we are content and free to do what we want. This idea of happiness cares not about whether the person experiencing it is growing and developing, but only that there is an escape from suffering.

God has paid us the compliment of loving us in the deepest and most tragic sense. He suffered the pain and separation of the death of His Son that we might have the choice of life and a relationship with Him. We are enjoined time and again in the Bible to identify with the pain of His sacrifice and death, and in so doing to experience the process of learning, growing, and developing into the person we are to become and all of what God wants us to be.

As I write these thoughts, our family is experiencing another time of grieving over the loss of a loved one. My grandson Ben Pollard died suddenly in his sleep on May 14, 2011. He was only twenty years old, a junior in college. Much of what life might bring was still ahead of him.

As I continue to grieve, some of those "why" questions still haunt me. Ben had been dating a beautiful young lady since high school. I know he loved her, but he will never have the joy of marriage or of raising a family as I have had. He had a compassionate care for the less fortunate. As he traveled with his dad in Latin America and with me in Africa, he saw some of the depths and sorrows of extreme poverty. He was determined to use his life to do something about it. That choice is now gone.

In my first book, *The Soul of the Firm*, I referred to my time with Ben at his birth to describe the potential in the birth of every child. Ben's was a difficult birth and he was a special miracle for all of us. As I looked at him as a baby boy who weighed only seven pounds and who fit in the cradle of my arm, I realized that all the potential of life was there, but for it to be realized there had to be care and investment by his parents and others. For twenty years, that care and investment was there. Early in his life, he made a commitment to choose Christ as his Savior. He still had some things to work out about what his response would be to some of the inequalities and unfairness in this world, but he had shown the heart and mind to serve others. Part of the unevenness of life is that God's way is not always our way. Ben is now enjoying God's presence, something I look forward to.

The next time I hug Ben will be in Heaven.

Much of what I have written so far reflects some of my experiences of the uneven nature of life. But you may be wondering how that relates to the broader questions that my grandson Ben was pondering: not only what's it all about relating to our own lives, but also how we should respond to the inequality and unfairness affecting so many others. As Ben would have put it, "Why do I have a soccer ball to play with when the kids living on the garbage dump in Guatemala City only have a fake ball made of plastic bags from the same garbage dump?"

Some of the unevenness of life in this world includes the inequality of opportunities to learn and to earn.

Learning to Learn

W. Edwards Deming, the noted authority on quality, reminded us that we have all been born with a curiosity to learn.

As people, whether children or adults, we need to be nurtured, encouraged, and motivated in our learning. We learn to accept and apply value systems as we relate to others in our homes, schools, and work environments. We exercise judgments within a framework of those values and have the capacity to love or hate, to care or hurt, to detract or contribute. We respond to recognition for a task well done. We grow in our self-esteem and well-being as we learn to serve and contribute to others. We are looking for purpose and meaning in what we do, whether it be in school or at work.

In a learning environment, there must be a focus on developing people's gifts and talents, not simply correcting their deficiencies. We should not equate learning only with what occurs in a school or define education by a diploma, a degree, or a lack thereof. We must never limit the educational process or orient the student to simply please the teacher by getting the right answers and avoiding mistakes.

Learning is a lifelong experience. We will never achieve a level of learning where we know all we should know.

Not everyone in the world has the opportunity we have in America for a structured and formal learning process. Neither has everyone in America had an equal opportunity to learn. Although this is part of our uneven world, I have found that the potential among those who want to learn is overwhelming and that there are those who have overcome the lack of formal education.

I wish you could have been with me in a one-room schoolhouse high in the Andes Mountains in Ecuador to watch and participate as children and their parents from a Quechua Indian tribe learned to read and write, not only in their native Quechua tongue, but also in Spanish and English.

Or traveled with me to Romania and seen the little ten-year-old boy struggling to speak my language as he asked a simple question: "What is it like to be free?"

Or traveled with me on a train from St. Petersburg, Russia, to Tallinn, Estonia, with a group of high school students from East Germany just at the time the Berlin Wall was coming down. As they spoke to me in English, they expressed concern and fear over what would happen to them with the coming of more freedom. Up to that point, when students graduated from high school, they were assigned jobs. Now they were going back home to a new system and would have to look for work. Did they have the skills to compete with their West German counterparts? They were eager to learn but not sure where to start.

Learning beyond the classroom occurs as we invest ourselves in teaching others.

Or been with me on the west side of Chicago at Francis Scott Key Elementary School in a mentorship program sponsored by ServiceMaster, where I had the opportunity to work with Jason, a third-grade student, and to be his mentor. Over the lunch hour, we worked on improving his reading skills. One of my roles was to help him understand the words he was reading. I can remember the time we came to the word *profit* and I asked Jason if he knew what that word meant. He looked at me with those big brown eyes and said, "Sure, that's what Grandma earns when she rents out the second-floor apartment."

Jason's class bubbling with excitement and eager to learn.

Jason had some obstacles to overcome resulting from the limitations of his environment. Statistics showed that many from his neighborhood who had gone before did not finish high school, much less attend college. With some encouragement and nurturing of his desire to learn, Jason and many others flourished as a result of our mentoring program. Ten years after we started our partnership with Francis Scott Key School, we had a celebration at ServiceMaster with those students who had been in the program and were now in college.

These experiences, which have occurred all over the world, have some common elements that should challenge each of us to be involved in the teaching-learning process. All these young people were eager to learn. All of them, no matter where they lived, wanted to learn more about reading and writing English. They all needed help in their learning beyond what could occur in their traditional classrooms. They all, in some way, represent the future.

Much has been said and written about our American educational process. I am not here to criticize, condemn, or applaud. I have been involved enough in the process to know that, without the participation of volunteers to support the professional educators, we will not be able to maintain our leadership role as a nation.

Involvement in the teaching/learning process can be a family affair and reach to faraway places.

We live in a world of opportunity. We also live in a global economy. It is a highly competitive environment. America is no longer the single dominant economic force. The issue is not one of protecting American jobs; it is whether we will be able to train and educate our young people with all they need to know to innovate and compete in a global economy.

We should not bemoan the fact that others in this world have achieved economic success or are our competitors. We should, instead, recognize the challenge and apply our efforts to training and developing the leaders we need for the twenty-first century. One of the advantages we have is that the trade language in every part of the world is our native tongue—English. We have an educational system that still encourages innovation and initiative. We have the rich heritage of a public school system based on the fundamental principles of equal access and local governance. However, the issues of the day, including dropouts and at-risk students, the lack of parental support, and the lack of financial resources, have the potential to impose unacceptable barriers to the learning process.

A partnership with Daystar University teaching management principles to a group of African entrepreneurs.

The ever-increasing cost of education, especially higher education, is also a major issue. We need to be more efficient and effective. As we have now moved to an information-based society and have the technology to communicate over the Internet, will we make the necessary changes to adjust to this new virtual world? Will we take the time to understand how this changes the learning process, including the ability to teach beyond the four walls of the classroom and without the need for hardcover books? If we don't make the necessary changes, the scarcity of resources will limit our ability to maintain a competitive edge.

As part of resolving this growing predicament, business firms must recognize the need to participate in the continuous learning process in the workplace and to increase their support of, and involvement with, educational institutions. There must be a growing partnership between businesses and traditional educational systems.

Using the technology of Skype to teach Chinese business leaders in Shanghai from a conference room in Chicago.

I believe we should recognize that the student is the worker, not the work product, and that the desired result is not a test score or a good playback machine, but instead the development of a person who:

- knows how to think, identify issues, seek solutions, and become a productive member of society;
- learns as an individual, not as an average of a national norm;

- learns to manage self and ego as part of working and serving others;
- learns more by having the opportunity to teach and not just the opportunity to listen;
- responds to motivation in the classroom just as he or she responds on the athletic field or in the work environment;
- seeks positive role models to learn about right and wrong and how to build relationships;
- learns regardless of age; and
- has the basic verbal, mathematical, and scientific literacy to survive in an information-based society.

As the former business leader of a firm that was fully committed to supporting the educational process, my message to the schools of America is to please look to both the students and their future employers as your customers. Listen to these customers as you review and change your curricula and set standards of effectiveness for your teachers.

As business leaders, we should also recognize that learning is a lifelong experience. We are not only in the business of producing needed goods and services, but we should also become a University of Work for our employees.

In conclusion, I refer the reader to a more recent and detailed study of our K-12 school system done by former Secretary of State Condoleezza Rice and former New York City Schools Chancellor Joel Klein and published by the Council on Foreign Relations. They conclude that our country is moving to a time of crisis because of our inability to prepare our young people to serve and compete in a global environment. Their study reveals that less than thirty percent of our high school graduates are adequately prepared to meet the challenges of the future. They also note that this comes at a time when there is a lack of social cohesion in our society. Our young people have a growing feeling they will not have the same opportunities as their parents. The study concludes that the system would do better if there was more choice by the "customer" resulting in a competitive environment.

The Stewardship of Wealth

Another area of unevenness in the world is wealth. If we use only an economic measurement, we know that the range of wealth is so great that the poorest people in America would be wealthy in many other countries or areas of the world.

Our history over the last century, and especially in the last twenty-five years, confirms that the free-market system, with appropriate checks and balances by government, is *the* most effective system at encouraging innovation and the creation of wealth.

But when talking about wealth in monetary terms, it is important to recognize it is not just a zero-sum game. Monetary wealth can be created or destroyed by forces of the market that are beyond the control of any one owner. The problem is that many of the discussions or theories regarding redistribution of wealth presuppose a zero-sum world, or that wealth is a tangible commodity and we need to develop a system that spreads it around more evenly. In our current economy, many American homeowners are experiencing the reality that wealth is not just a commodity as they compare the current value of their homes with their mortgage balances. The wealth of "equity" that was once there is now gone. Values have dropped, and their homes are no longer financial assets on their balance sheets, but may in fact be net liabilities.

Wealth can also be destroyed by systems of government, even though they may have a stated egalitarian purpose of seeking to provide a more equal distribution of wealth. As governments seek to control or own economic and business resources in order to provide a more even playing field for all citizens, they can actually destroy wealth. To manage what they own and control, they often impose burdensome and inefficient bureaucracy that discourages innovation, risk-taking, and the making of investments for the future. The cumulative result is the destruction of wealth and the increase of poverty, with only a small elite benefitting from their privileged political position.

The collapse of the Soviet Union is a classic example. I had the opportunity to visit the Soviet Union and Eastern Europe in the fall of 1989, during the initial period of *glasnost* and *perestroika* and just as the Berlin Wall was coming down. I was traveling with my son Chip, my brother-in-law Don Soderquist (who was then vice-chairman and chief operating officer of Walmart), and his two sons, Mark and Jeff. We spent nine days and traveled thirty-five hundred miles by train from Warsaw, Poland, to Moscow and Leningrad (now St. Petersburg) in the Soviet Union, and then to Tallinn, Estonia; Riga, Latvia; Vilnius, Lithuania; and back to Warsaw.

The principal purpose of our trip was to visit with local Christian groups to encourage them and to share in their financial support. In addition, we visited with officials from the Ministry of Health in Moscow, learning about the possibility of ServiceMaster serving hospitals in the Soviet Union. We also participated in an event sponsored by the Soviet Science Institute and presented Walmart and ServiceMaster as examples of companies doing business in a free-enterprise system. It was a life-changing experience.

My first impression of Warsaw was a drab, dirty international airport, with the only evidence of color being a sign advertising a new casino. After going through customs, we were met by John, a leader in one of the local churches. He was our guide as we spent time that evening visiting members of the local church, sharing in song, testimony, and prayer. The next day, we toured the old city of Warsaw, saw the monument to the memory of the massacre that occurred in the Jewish ghetto during World War II, and spent time listening and learning about what it was like to live in Poland, which included long lines for food and clothing. Inflation was rampant, with prices of food and petrol rising weekly. There were long waits, measured in years, to secure an apartment or a telephone if one already had an apartment. The economy was a mess and people were in survival mode.

The local Christians were excited about their new freedom to worship and evangelize, but frustrated with their limited resources. Property ownership was now possible in Poland, and there was an opportunity to purchase some property in the country for a camp ministry, but where would the capital to do so come from?

The scheduled eighteen-hour trip to Moscow took more than twenty hours. Russian trains were not usually pictures of comfort. They were heated by coal stoves that sometimes did not work. There was no food and only lukewarm tea. Four to a compartment made for close quarters. The blankets and pillows had been around for a long time and carried a distinct smell of body odors.

We were able to discuss with some of our fellow passengers the important issues of life, such as what they would die for, whether they knew where they were going after death, and whether they had a relationship with God. There were also times when we just looked out the window to see the fields draped in snow, forests of tall evergreens, small wooden houses, and not much evidence of human activity. The cold of the Russian winter was readily apparent.

When we finally arrived in Moscow, we found a city bustling with people, cars, and buses; long lines in stores with empty shelves; cabdrivers, waiters, and others openly criticizing the government and the system; and hotel clerks in a position to help but with no training or motivation to do so. The dollar was definitely in demand, with many refusing services unless payment was made in "hard currency." Price controls were still in place, with not just daily but hourly changes in the foreign exchange rate for the ruble. The cost of a subway ride was less than a penny; a two-bedroom apartment rented for less than $6 a month; a five-course meal cost less than $1.50 per person.

Most of the buildings were in a state of disrepair. I never saw a clean floor in Moscow. The standard mop for the chambermaid consisted of a wooden T-frame with a dirty rag wrapped around it, which she dipped in a bucket of dirty water. Although we were in a modern, scientific society, we were warned not to drink the water because of contamination. However, there were isolated

The Tides of Life

examples of free enterprise, including young merchants hawking their wares behind the Kremlin walls in a so-called shopping center consisting of separate huts and stalls in an open area.

Red Square is a symbol of the use and abuse of power.

Our two visits to Red Square were filled with emotion. For most of my lifetime, Russia had been one of those places people talked about but knew little of. My vision had been limited to Red Square and the Kremlin Wall, the seat of power of the enemy. Here we were in the cold and the snow, seeing the size and the magnitude of it all. We had to pinch ourselves to believe we were there. It caused a response, and together we sang the hymn "He Is Lord," much to the amazement of the Russians passing by.

The next day, we had our meeting with the Ministry of Health to explore the opportunity of ServiceMaster serving in Russia. The deputy minister was cordial yet stiff. He acknowledged that there were few hospitals in Moscow that would meet the U.S. standards and agreed there were growing problems of motivation and training among service workers. We concluded our time with an invitation for him to visit us when he came to the United States.

Our meeting in the afternoon at the Academy of Science was stimulating. After a review of our two businesses, we received an enthusiastic response and encouragement to bring our businesses to the Soviet Union. There would be tax incentives and a reduced requirement of participation by government in ownership. But our questions as to currency exchange and repatriation of profits were not easily answered. Neither did the officials want to respond to our brief experiences with the black market or the issue of corruption.

That evening, we spent time with Christians at a Baptist church. There were more than six hundred in attendance. They proudly displayed pictures from the Billy Graham Crusade in Hungary and prayed for his future visit to Russia.

The next day, we traveled to Leningrad, now renamed St. Petersburg. The beauty of the city was apparent, even though it was cold. It has been called the "Venice of the North," and our visit provided us the chance to learn something of Russian life before Communism. At the Winter Palace of the czar and at many of the beautiful churches, there was evidence of individual creativity and art, including many paintings depicting stories of our Christian faith, from the birth to the death and resurrection of Jesus Christ. The visit with the local Christians was warm and encouraging. They were conducting seminars in evangelism as we arrived. The pastor seemed to have a keen sense of mission and ministry.

The next stop on our journey was Tallinn, Estonia. We worshipped on Sunday morning in the Baptist church in the old city. St. Olaf's Church was more than seven hundred years old. Under Communist rule, the building had not been used for many years and had fallen into disrepair. However, use of it had finally been given to a Baptist group, and they had done a beautiful job of restoration.

Our visits in Latvia and Lithuania were short, but we were once again encouraged with the vision and work of the Christian church.

As our trip neared an end, we realized that everywhere we had been there was openness and the people were thirsty to learn more about the West. In every church we attended, there was a need for more Bibles. There also appeared to be a great opportunity for the distribution of Christian literature. We experienced no restrictions in our travel or in our visits or contacts. It appeared that Soviet Premier Mikhail Gorbachev's vision of *glasnost* and *perestroika* was for a Soviet Union that would be more open and honest about its problems but still sufficiently centralized to remain a powerful Communist state. However, as history has confirmed, he could not pull it off. Seventy years of a godless system that sought to centralize and control the means of production had resulted in the destruction of wealth. The people were poor in their pocketbooks and, for many, also poor in their souls. The Soviet Union was bankrupt and could not survive, and so were many of the political and economic systems of Eastern Europe.

When there is abuse of power, people suffer.

As I point out some of the problems relating to theories or systems that suggest there is a macro solution for a more equal distribution of wealth, I also confess that, as a Christian, I am still uncomfortable with the fairness or justice of the current disparity of wealth in America and the rest of the world. But I also confess that I have no human macro solution. In Peter Drucker's words,

"It may be possible to make the world more tolerable, but don't look for great improvements."

I doubt we will ever have an effective human system that addresses the problem of the distribution of wealth to everyone's satisfaction and still encourages the initiative, innovation, and risk-taking necessary for the creation of wealth. The grand experiment today in China, which is seeking to marry centralized government control with a free-market system, has resulted in an increase in the average income of its people but has not resolved the growing gap of wealth between the "haves" and the "have nots."

The answer for me is not to be found in a macro solution but in what should be my individual response. That response should not be limited to a monetary or economic solution. There is also a poverty of the soul that needs to be considered. This leads me to a series of questions: What is important in life? Do I know and understand the difference between needs and wants? Do I know and understand what it means to sacrifice? What are my responsibilities as a follower of Jesus Christ to help in meeting the needs of others?

Blessings and Responsibilities

As I have pondered these questions over a period of time and sought guidance from God and His Word, the development of my response was influenced by yet another trip. In 1995, my wife and I traveled to the Middle East (Jordan and Egypt) and then to Eastern Europe (Romania, Slovakia, and Hungary). The trip included visiting with missionary friends and our ServiceMaster partners in Jordan; launching a new business in Cairo; seeing and learning from the antiquities of ancient Egypt; participating in a graduation ceremony at a new college in Romania; and visiting with several entrepreneurs in Eastern Europe who had started their businesses with the help of a small venture fund Judy and I had established several years before.

We met people from all walks of life: those in positions of power and wealth, and those who had no place to call home other than a tent and a desert floor. We were overwhelmed by the accomplishments and wealth of ancient Egypt and were perplexed by what motivated a society to dedicate itself to building great edifices of stone to house mummified bodies of past leaders. It involved their view of life after death—a life that could be enjoyed only by the select few who had wealth and who ruled over the people.

The pyramids are among the "Seven Wonders of the Ancient World." They have lasted for centuries. We admired the skill and intelligence of those who designed them and directed their construction. But what about those who built them? What were their lives like? How did they prepare for eternity? Who were their gods? Were most of them slaves? Were some of them Jewish slaves building for the pharaoh and forced to make bricks without straw, suffering and sacrificing, waiting for the day of exodus, when Moses would stand up and say, "Let my people go"?

What a challenge of leadership for Moses—over two million people to be led across the Red Sea and through the barren wilderness. A journey that would normally take approximately two years wound up taking forty.

I was able to stand at the top of Mount Nebo with the wind in my face and look over the fertile Jordan Valley, with the Dead Sea to my left and Jericho straight ahead (due west). I was viewing that Promised Land from the same mountain where God had brought Moses to see the land he would never enter. He had a dream, a vision that would be fulfilled not by him but by his successor, Joshua.

As I stood there, I thought of my dreams. Many of them God had allowed me to see fulfilled. As I reflected upon my blessings, I was also reminded of all the people I had seen who were caught up in the poverty of the present. What were their dreams? Why wasn't I born among the thousands of people living on the garbage dumps of Cairo? Why did I have the opportunity to be born, grow up, be educated, practice law, raise my family, and conduct business in "the land of the free and home of the brave"?

I did not have the same struggles as my colleagues in Romania or Slovakia, who had been born and raised in a land corrupted by Communism and who struggled to eke out a living in a third-world economy in the face of high inflation rates and corrupt and unstable governments. They were growing their businesses, developing their people, and making a profit, but facing problems I never had to confront.

A few days later, I gave the commencement address at Emanuel University of Oradea, Romania. I saw the enthusiasm among the graduates who had had the opportunity to be educated in a Christian university—an opportunity that had not been available ten years earlier. What is fair? What is just? Are the opportunities of one person and the limitations of another just the luck of the draw? And for those of us who have been blessed with so much, is all of what we have an asset or a liability? Sometimes it just gets in the way. We can be consumed by what we have or become envious and dwell on what we don't have instead of focusing on the needs of others. Sometimes we get so caught up with our own importance and the importance of our titles, positions, or schedules that there is no time to serve, to reflect, or to develop a relationship with others.

A time of commencement at Emanuel University. With freedom comes the opportunity to learn and be productive.

On the way from Amman to Petra in Jordan, we stopped on the side of the road to visit with some Bedouin children tending their flock of sheep and goats. Soon their father invited us to join them in his tent. The men were invited to the front of the tent, the women to the back. We sat on rugs stretched over the sand and sipped tea from unwashed cups. I was reminded that this tent and surroundings were much like what Abraham experienced over three thousand years ago.

For this Bedouin, however, there was not much of a future for his lifestyle. The cost of feed had outstripped the market price for his sheep and goats. He might soon have to abandon the freedom of a nomad and move into a town or village and get a job.

Lessons from a Bedouin with a heart to serve.

He was a very gracious host. He even invited us to stay for lunch, but being unsure of what had gone into the stew cooking over the fire and with a schedule to be in Petra by early afternoon, we declined and went on our way. Was I too busy to stay and learn more from this Bedouin and his family? Was my stomach too sensitive to eat his cooking? Did I care enough about him as a person created in the image of God to accept his hospitality and begin the process of friendship, or was I more worried about keeping the schedule?

If he had come to my house on his camel, would I have invited this stranger dressed in robes and sandals into my home? Would I have washed his dirty feet? Would I have offered him lunch? What is important in life? Am I willing to sacrifice myself and my precious time for another? For someone different from me? And yes, in so doing, to share my faith with that person?

When we arrived home from this trip, Judy and I were greeted with two weeks of unopened mail. Within the pile was a special letter from a missionary doctor working in the mountains of Bolivia among the Quechua Indians. He told of a grueling two-day journey he had taken on a motorbike over mountain roads and narrow passes, and across fields and streams to visit a sick patient. When he arrived, he found a woman with a cancerous tumor in her throat. She was near death. Her treatment required immediate surgery, but that was out of the question because there was no nearby hospital. He was frustrated. He was qualified to do the job. He had traveled a long way to get there, but in the end he did not have the necessary tools. This experience caused him to ask some of these same questions. What is fair? What is important? Is the sacrifice of my life and family for service to others worth it? What's it all about?

For Dr. Steve and for me, the source for the answers to these questions is God and His Word, the Bible. Jesus said: "Any of you who does not give up everything he has cannot be my disciple" (Luke 14:33, NIV); "For what does it profit a man if he gains the whole world and loses or forfeits himself?" (Luke 9:25); "It is easier for a camel to go through the eye of a needle than for a rich man to enter the kingdom of God" (Luke 18:25, NIV); "If then you have not been faithful in the unrighteous wealth, who will entrust to you the true riches?" (Luke 16:11); "Whoever would be great among you must be your servant, and whoever would be first among you must be slave of all. For even the Son of Man [Jesus Christ] came not to be served but to serve, and to give His life as a ransom for many" (Mark 10:43–45).

These words of Jesus were summarized by the Apostle Paul in the conclusion of his first letter to Timothy:

> Command those who are rich in this present world not to be arrogant nor to put their hope in wealth, which is so uncertain, but to put their hope in God, Who richly provides us with everything for our enjoyment. Command them to do good, to be rich in good deeds, and to be generous and willing to share. (1 Timothy 6:17–18, NIV)

So, what's it all about? What is important in life? What is fair? What is just? Is there room for sacrifice? I have concluded the only reason I have something that somebody else doesn't have, whether that something is money, possessions, education, talent, or opportunity, is not for me to own or control it, but to use, share, or invest it so that it will increase and be of benefit to others. My role is that of a steward or trustee, not an owner. God is the owner. Doing good is not to win favor with God or to earn my way to Heaven; instead, it is part of my responsibility and obligation to act within God's plan of fairness with eternity in view.

As C. S. Lewis reminded us:

> [God] could, if He chose, repair our bodies miraculously without food; or give us food without the aid of farmers, bakers, and butchers; or knowledge without the aid of learned men; or convert the heathen without missionaries. Instead, He allows soils and weather and animals and the muscles, minds, and wills of men to co-operate in the execution of His will. . . . For He seems to do nothing of Himself that He can possibly delegate to His creatures. . . . We are either privileged to share in the game or compelled to collaborate in the work. Is this how (no light matter) God makes something—indeed, makes gods—out of nothing?

The reality is that God has chosen us to accomplish His will, and so a value and worth (we might even say a wealth) is produced as we exercise true stewardship, become productive, and invest our time, talent, and treasure in the lives of others. All that we have and are demands an investment. We are not just to spend it on ourselves or waste it. There is no personal accumulation plan with God. "To whom much has been given, much will be required" (Luke 12:48, NRSV); "For you know the grace of our Lord Jesus Christ, that though He was rich, yet for your sakes He became poor, so that you through His poverty might become rich" (2 Corinthians 8:9, NIV).

God has provided me many unique opportunities to exercise responsible choices. ServiceMaster was certainly one of those opportunities. It allowed me to develop my gifts and talents. It provided for my family and enabled Judy and me to share and invest in the lives of many people. I owe much to those who went before and who set the vision, mission, and purpose of the company, as well as to those I worked with who made it happen every day. My commitment to them went beyond self-interest. I desired to build upon what we had and to provide even greater opportunities for those who would follow. Our ownership in ServiceMaster has also provided Judy and me the resources to invest in and serve with many organizations doing God's work in meeting the needs of people and sharing His love and His desire to have a relationship with them.

My prayer has been, and continues to be, that I will run the race of life in such a way that when it is over, my barns will be empty and my investments in sharing and serving will be completed.

A Poem and a Letter

I close this chapter with a poem and a letter. I found the poem in my father's Bible soon after his death. It has been a continuing reminder of my role in a broken and uneven world—to not only be an example and to invest in others, but also to do likewise with my children. I wrote the letter to my children on a return trip from Japan as I reflected upon some of the principles of family life in this uneven world.

A careful man I want to be,
    a little fellow follows me;
I do not want to go astray,
    for fear he'll go the self-same way.
I cannot once escape his eyes,
    what ere he sees me do, he tries,
Like me he says he's going to be,
    the little chap who follows me.
He thinks that I am good and fine,
    believes in every word of mine;
The base in me he must not see,
    the little chap who follows me.
I must remember as I go,
    through summer's sun and winter's snow;
I am building for the years to be,
    the little chap who follows me.

Dear Family,

I am writing you this letter on my way home from Tokyo. This brief time in Japan confirmed for me, once again, the size and diversity of our world and the many people who live in it. How thankful I am to be born and raised by Christian parents in America and how frustrated I am at my seeming inability to have much of a spiritual impact on some of my business associates in Japan. But what a joy it was to see the business and spiritual growth of one of our Christian managers. Tomita-san stands tall.

Life is a continuing struggle—a war if you will between the forces of good and evil. Before leaving home, I was able to complete J. R. R. Tolkein's *The Lord of the Rings.* Thank you, Chip, for the encouragement to do so. What a story. Three cheers for Frodo. He suffered a pain that would never leave and gave up a ring of power that grew faster than he did. In the end, he lost what he could not keep and gained what he could not buy. Oh for a friend like Sam and to experience the work of the Spirit of God in our lives with a touch of the supernatural that was represented by Gandalf.

As one grows older, thoughts about the end of this life or that shore by the crystal sea become more of a reality. To have a mission and to have completed that mission is that great calling. A calling from above. A calling from God.

Since I am in the mood of reflections on life, here are some thoughts for you:

1. Mother is a wonderful partner. Our love for each other has continued to allow for the smoothing of the rough edges. Before our journey is over, there may be a need for one of us to love with no anticipated response and only a memory of what went on before. Enclosed is an article we have shared together by Dr. McQuilken. His wife is suffering from Alzheimer's. He expresses total unselfish love. Love that flows not only from the heart, but from the covenant he made for better, for worse, in sickness and in health, until death do us part.

2. Each of you has begun your own family unit. The growth and spiritual development of your family is a mission in life. Commit yourself to it. During this trip, I have treasured the picture of our extended family and thank God for you and the contribution you have made to me and my life.

3. "If we confess our sins, He is faithful and just to forgive our sins." The experience of forgiveness is essential to emotional health and spiritual growth. God seeks to be involved in the process. Go to Him on a regular basis to review and confess your shortcomings and sins. In my life, the Communion service every Sunday morning has been an important, disciplined call for confession and forgiveness and renewal. "So let a man examine himself and then eat."

4. Bloom where you are planted and give it all you have got. God has each of you in different experiences—work, home, and otherwise. There may be some imperfections in what you are doing, but there is no task too small or too mundane that it should be done without the striving for excellence.

Do not minimize the struggle of life. There is the force of evil in this world. The currents of life are often uneven. Keep your eye above. Direct your thoughts on Him from where your strength cometh.

Love, your Dad

The crooked roads shall become straight,
  the rough ways smooth.
And all mankind will see God's salvation.
  (Luke 3:5–6, NIV)

3

Work—a Calling or a Curse?

Whatever you do, do it all for the glory of God.

1 CORINTHIANS 10:31, NIV

Does a framework of life affect our view of work and the choices we make about work? Why should we work? Is there a purpose for our work? What if we can't work or if we are unemployed? Can the work I do contribute to the kind of person I am becoming? Does some work have a higher value than other work? Is some work sacred and other work secular? Is work a calling or a curse?

Why Work

Work has been defined by some as "an effort to do something." There was work at the beginning of creation. In Genesis 1 we read: "In the beginning, God created the heavens and the earth" (v. 1), and "God created man in His own image, in the image of God He created him; male and female He created them" (v. 27). At the end of this creation story, it says: "And God saw everything that He had made, and behold, it was very good. . . . God finished His work that He had done, and He rested" (1:31; 2:2). God exerted Himself to do the work of creation and then rested. Work and rest go together.

But the story goes on. Adam and Eve, the people God created in His own image with freedom of choice and who were representative of all humankind, chose to disobey God. As a result, God cursed the ground because of their disobedience and said: "Through painful toil you will eat of it all the days of your life. It will produce thorns and thistles for you, and you will eat the plants of the field. By the sweat of your brow you will eat your food until you return to the ground, since from it you were taken; for dust you are and to dust you will return" (3:17–19, NIV).

Are we to conclude that, in God's order of things, work is the result of sin and that toil and sorrow in work should be the norm, not the exception? If so, then we may also concur with the writer of Ecclesiastes, who said: "What does a man get for all the toil and anxious striving with which he labors under the sun? All his days his work is pain and grief; even at night his mind does not rest. This too is meaningless" (2:22–23, NIV).

But is this view of work as a "curse" consistent with the account of God's work at creation?

We are reminded by the Apostle Paul in his letter to the Colossians: "Whatever you do, work at it with all your heart" (3:23, NIV). Paul condemned idleness and used his own work of tent-making as an example for others. The Bible is written for a workaday world and describes a place where both God and the people He created are active at work. The Bible is a book by workers about workers and for workers. So it is not work itself that is condemned by the curse. In fact, we are enjoined by Scripture to do both good works and good work.

The reality is that work will involve toil. At times, it will be hard and difficult. Physical labor will often involve the "sweat of our brow." There can be stress in our work—physical and mental. There will be times when we fail in our work. There can be both good work and evil work.

But toil in work does not have to result in drudgery. As Dorothy Sayers put it in her classic essay *Why Work?*, work can be:

. . . a way of life in which the nature of man should find its proper exercise and delight and so fulfill itself to the glory of God. That should, in fact, be thought of as a creative activity, undertaken for the love of the work itself; and that man, made in God's image, should make things, as God makes them, for the sake of doing well a thing that is worth doing.

A View from History

As part of your framework of life, you may not agree with the biblical account of creation and your starting point for a view of work may not begin with God. However, we all should be able to agree that Western thought and views of work have, over the centuries, been profoundly influenced by the Judeo-Christian tradition, as well as some ideas of early Greek philosophers, including Plato and Aristotle. For the Greeks, the concept of dualism included the belief that there were higher and lower dimensions of ideas and work activities. This view would later influence early church leaders to distinguish between work that was sacred and work that was secular.

Over time, a view developed that characterized tasks related to the support of the church as holy and all other work as mundane, worldly, and of no redeeming value. The holy tasks were consistent with the work of God and the mundane tasks involved the work that had been cursed by God.

There followed the monastic movement, with its aesthetic craving for simplicity in food, dress, and shelter, and for freedom from entanglements with the secular world. For those who chose this separated life with its simple but hard work, there could be hope of reconciling a man's labor with his calling from God. Some encouraged this basic work ethic to apply not only to the monks in the monastery but to all Christians and to all work. But as time went on, the distinction between sacred and secular work was reinforced. This distinction was emphasized in the writings of Thomas Aquinas as he developed a hierarchy of work, with spiritual works ranking higher than manual works in their contribution to the lives of men. Only spiritual work was edifying to God. All other work was morally neutral.

With the Protestant Reformation came a re-emphasis on the integration of faith and work at all levels and a conception that all work was endowed with virtue. "A housemaid who does her work is no further away from God than a priest in the pulpit," said Martin Luther. According to this view, every man is "called," not just a few, and every place is invested with a potential for godliness, not just the church. Luther rejected the view that so-called worldly duties should be subordinated to holy duties.

John Calvin expanded the view of work as a vocation, or a calling of God. It was more than a series of tasks. It also involved a duty and an obligation. One's work was to be done in a way that would glorify God. It was seen as a fulfillment of God's purposes and was no longer viewed as a deterrent to a relationship with God. Instead, work came to be regarded as essential to complete that relationship. Thus, one was able to enrich his or her faith within the context of "faith without works is dead" (James 2:26, KJV) by doing good work as well as good works.

John Wesley concluded that there was an inherent tension between productive work and religion. Religion, he said, encouraged productivity and frugality, which in turn produced riches and wealth. But he also observed that as wealth grew, the essence of what religion should be in the hearts and minds of people and in their relationship to God and others typically diminished. His answer was a series of simple exhortations: *"Gain all you can," "Save all you can,"* and *"Give all you can."*

The Puritans went a step further by emphasizing the relationship between man's work and stewardship responsibilities. People were encouraged to seek the kind of work that would be most productive. If one failed in his search or chose the less productive way, one would not be a good steward of God's gifts. Thus, a person could labor to be rich for God but not for self. Wealth was ethically corrupt only insofar as it was a temptation to idleness and to a sinful enjoyment of life.

This standard became the basis for the spirit of capitalism in early America. One's work, the effort to earn money, was an expression of virtue and came with a duty and an obligation to use one's talent and resources as a steward for God.

Modern Views

If this was the origin and heritage of the spirit of capitalism in America, what can be said of that spirit today? Max Weber, in his book *The Protestant Ethic and the Spirit of Capitalism*, concludes that by the beginning of the twentieth century, any relationship between religious belief and the conduct of business was generally absent. The worker, he said, was part of a machine of production caught in an "iron cage" without hope of relating his work to the process of human development or glorifying God.

In more recent times, George Gilder, in his book *Wealth and Poverty*, poses the question as follows: "Can men live in a free society if they have no reason to believe that it is also a just society?" He concludes that there need to be moral and meaningful criteria for a fairer distribution of power, privilege, and property. He goes on to say that the conclusion of some is that capitalism is morally vacant and can perpetuate gross immorality, such as racism, sexism, inequality, and environmental abuse. Can work in such a system be a calling of God?

What are some of the views people have about their work today?

Some people view work as a necessary evil. Work is not intended to edify and is often onerous. I have no choice about what I should do. I just have to work at any job I can find because I need to support my family. Without work, I simply cannot survive. With this mind-set, one often approaches work with a certain air of contempt, a put-upon attitude that can permeate the way in which the task is completed.

Others view work as a means to an end. This view is described by Robert Michaelsen as "the American gospel of work." The basic affirmation is that hard work will provide all that I need in life, with the "needs" being described as power, social status, money, and wealth, or some combination of these. Thus, I work because I want a better life, which can be measured in the size of my home, my bank account, my title, or my authority. This motivational ladder of success can generate frustration. One who accepts this view can always be striving but never attaining because at each new rung of the ladder there is still a higher rung to climb.

For some, work is something they enjoy because it uses their skills and talents. It enables them to be productive and excel at what they do, and also earn enough money to support their families.

Others may become so engrossed in their work that it becomes an end in itself, and so the modern-day workaholic is born. Work becomes a habit and, more than that, an obsession. It turns family, friends, and even recreation into afterthoughts.

Then there are those who react to the emptiness of work measured solely in monetary terms by seeking an alternative in leisure. Work then becomes a means to the end of leisure. Where I work, how long I work, and whether my work hours can be scheduled to accommodate my required leisure time and recreational activities become the overriding factors in determining whether I have a good job.

Then there are those who continue to view certain work as a special or holy calling, a sacred ministry. They often refer to a minister or missionary as one who has been called to full-time church or Christian service. Their work has been sanctified by God's blessing and often involves a monetary sacrifice, with rewards that will be received in Heaven rather than here on earth. Those who do other kinds of work are classified as laymen, unworthy of performing sacramental duties.

So we have seen from the flow of history, first an attitude that considered work to be at worst a curse and, later, that considered secular work to be morally neutral at best. Man's attitude toward work gradually progressed to a position that recognized all good work could be involved in God's calling. Finally, we have arrived at the modern-day view, which has lost much of this message, and where, for many, the focus on the materialistic accomplishments of one's work is exceeded only by one's frustration for failing to achieve it.

The basic questions of why—Why do I work? Why do I earn money?—are answered without regard to God and His purpose for those He created. For some, there is no God. For others, God may have a bearing on whether they are honest or dependable, but beyond that point, faith in God has no place in a workaday world. It is faith on Sunday and work on Monday.

However, there also seems to be a growing number of people who reject this bifurcation of the sacred and secular and view their so-called secular work as a ministry and a calling of God. They see work as an opportunity to integrate the claims of their faith with the demands of their work; to excel at what they do in honor of the God they love; and to, in the words of Dorothy Sayers, view work as not "primarily, a thing one does to live, but the thing one lives to do."

A Purpose and Meaning for Work

For most of us, work is not a solo occupation. More often than not, we work with others in an organization that has common objectives. We contribute and cooperate with others in accomplishing these objectives. Our work involves developing relationships with people, and usually there develops an interdependency in this relationship. We need to know, trust, and complement each other. We often work in teams. Sometimes we find ourselves in positions of management or leadership. Many of us work in organizations that conduct businesses that produce goods and services for a profit. Where does our framework of life and faith fit into such a community?

I must admit that I didn't think much about these questions and the purpose and meaning of work until I joined ServiceMaster.

As you already know from the first chapter, I practiced law and served as an administrator and college professor before joining ServiceMaster. I knew God had led me into the practice of law. It was my desire to excel in my representation of clients and to earn a living and support my family. During that time, I was active in my church and served as a Sunday school teacher and elder. And while I sought to honor God in the way I practiced law, it was still the practice of law, with all of the nitty-gritties that went into a secular profession.

As I will explain further in the next chapter, my desire to go to Wheaton College was clearly a calling of God. It was a Christian college, a faith-based community, and there was an open door for me to integrate the claims of my faith with the demands of my work. However, there was no challenge from the college community in so doing, because it was the accepted norm there.

ServiceMaster, however, was a different story. It was a for-profit business that was making a good profit and growing very rapidly. It was a public company whose stock was traded at a high multiple. There would be an opportunity for me, as an employee, to not only earn a living, but to generate some wealth from the stock I would own.

But ServiceMaster was more than just a business serving customers, making money, and creating wealth for its shareholders. It also had a mission and purpose that included honoring God and developing people.

You have already been introduced to Ken Hansen and Ken Wessner. Each in his own way saw business and his work in the firm and the marketplace as a ministry, a calling of God.

The two Kens wanted me to come to the firm and initially head up the legal and financial affairs of the company, reporting directly to Ken Wessner. During the recruiting process, they had shared their vision for the future and inferred that someday I might have an opportunity to lead the company. So, as I came to that final day of decision about whether I would join the ServiceMaster team and as I sat in Ken Hansen's office waiting to sign the final documents of employment, I decided I needed to know more about exactly what I would have to do to be CEO of this company.

Ken Wessner and Ken Hansen were mentors and role models who viewed their work in the marketplace as a calling of God and a ministry to those they served.

I started pressing the two Kens on their expectations and how long it would take for me to be considered for president and CEO. After about five minutes of listening, Ken Hansen stood up, looked me in the eye, and said, "Bill, the interview is over."

As I was ushered to the front door and left ServiceMaster that morning, I concluded I had blown my opportunity and this was God's way of directing me back to the practice of law.

Two days later, Ken Hansen called and asked me if I wanted to know what had happened in his office that day. I said that I did, and we met for breakfast the next morning. Ken's words to me were simply put: "Bill, if you want to come to ServiceMaster and contribute, you will have a great career. But if you are coming to the company for a title or a position or to promote yourself, you'd better forget it."

Ken then proceeded to share the meaning and role of being a servant leader in a public company and how the doing of business could be a calling of God. There were lessons for me to learn, including: (1) Never give a title or position to someone who can't live without it. (2) Determine up front whether the leader's self-interest or the interest of others would come first. (3) Know whether, as a leader, you are willing to do what you ask others to do. (4) Know whether you, as a leader, have the heart and commitment to develop people, not only in what they are doing but also in the people they are becoming.

I made the decision that day to join the ServiceMaster team. Ken soon tested my commitment, and also took time to teach me what it was like to walk in the shoes of the people I would lead. During the first eight weeks as a corporate vice president, I spent my days with the service workers, doing the service tasks we performed for our customers. I learned the reality of my dependence upon and responsibility to the people I would lead. Little did I realize then that this would ultimately involve over two hundred thousand people as we grew to serve over ten million customers in forty-five countries. This experience often reminded me of my own imperfections and my need to admit my mistakes, ask for forgiveness, and seek guidance from above.

Later in my career, when I became CEO of the firm, the faces of our service workers would often flash across my mind as I dealt with those inevitable judgment calls between the rights and wrongs of running a business. The integrity of my actions had to pass their scrutiny. Otherwise, I was deceiving myself and those I was committed to serve and failing to honor God in my work.

The bottom line for people seeking to integrate their faith with their work is the people you work with. Every one of them has been created in the image and likeness of God, with his or her own fingerprint of potential. You are, and they are, in the process of becoming someone, and, yes, the work environment has an influence on who you and they are becoming. It is a growth process that is either moving in a positive or negative direction. And, yes, if we live normal life spans, we will spend most of our waking hours in our work environments.

Ken Hansen often reminded us at ServiceMaster of one of his favorite quotes from C. S. Lewis:

> There are no *ordinary* people. You have never talked to a mere mortal. Nations, cultures, arts, civilisations—these are mortal, and their life is to ours as the life of a gnat. But it is the immortals whom we joke with, work with, marry, snub, and exploit.

The Question of God

It is important to recognize that, although a successful business firm makes a meaningful contribution to the economy and welfare of the communities in which it functions, creates wealth and jobs, and pays taxes for the support of a functioning government, no business firm is eternal. Only people have an eternal existence beyond this life. How, then, do we, as workers, managers, or leaders in business, take this truth and make a difference? How can we affirm our faith but not impose it?

At ServiceMaster, we decided to be overt about the issue as we raised the question of God in our mission statement.

Our company objectives were simply stated: "To Honor God in All We Do; To Help People Develop; To Pursue Excellence; and To Grow Profitably." Those first two objectives were "end goals"; the second two were "means goals." We did not use that first objective as a basis for exclusion. It was, in fact, the reason for our promotion of diversity, as we recognized that different people with different beliefs were all part of God's work. Neither should one conclude that the first objective was simply an expression of American evangelical thought, a reflection of a denominational belief, or advocacy of the free-enterprise system wrapped in a religious blanket. It was, instead, a response to the fundamental question of life, which transcends all cultures and economic or political systems: "Is there a God and, if so, what is my relationship to Him?" It was an affirmative statement that there was a purpose for life and for work, and there was a reason for people to work and invest their lives in the growth and development of others.

As a business firm, we wanted to excel at generating profits and creating value for our shareholders. If we didn't want to play by these rules, we didn't belong in the ballgame. But we also tried to encourage an environment where the workplace could be an open community wherein questions about the existence of God, about a person's moral and spiritual development, and about how one related the claims of his or her faith with work were issues of discussion, debate, learning, and understanding. We considered the people of our firm to be the soul of the firm.

This did not mean that everything was done right. We made our share of mistakes. We sometimes failed and did things wrong. But because of a stated standard, and a reason for that standard, we could not hide our mistakes. Mistakes were regularly flushed out into the open for correction and, in some cases, for forgiveness. Leaders could not protect themselves at the expense of those they were leading.

Neither was our way of doing business a standard that could be used as a simplistic reason for our financial success. It could not be applied like a mathematical formula. It did, however, provide a foundation and a reference point for action. It was a living set of principles that allowed us to confront the difficult failures that are part of life and to work with the assurance that the starting point never changed but provided a reason and hope for everything.

As we sought to apply these principles in the work environment, it required linking the performance of the task with the development of the people performing the task. Management was not just getting the right things done through others. It also involved what was happening to people in the process and who they were becoming in their work. The task as defined, the tool as designed, and the training as provided all had to contribute to, not detract from, the workers doing their work and achieving a result they could be proud of. As we raised these questions about the worker and the work, they became self-energizing and resulted in a correcting and improving process that was never complete. It was our basis for continuous improvement as we sought excellence in serving our customers.

So for us, business was not a game of manipulation that accomplished a series of tasks for a profit, with the gain going to a few at the top and with the atrophy of the soul of the people producing the results. People were not just economic animals or non-personal production units. Every person had his or her own dignity, personality, and potential. Only people, not machines, can respond to the unexpected and surprise the customer with extraordinary service. Only people can serve. Only people can lead. Only people can innovate and create.

Frankly, when you view the person as only a production unit or as something that can be defined solely in economic terms, motivation or incentive schemes have a tendency to be mechanical and manipulative. The drive to design a system that will "idiot-proof" the process will, in turn, make people feel like idiots.

Fortune magazine described the soulless company as suffering from "enemies within," and cited Henry Ford's quote: "Why is it that I always get the whole person when all I really wanted was a pair of hands?" A soulless adversarial environment should not be the model for the future.

Samuel Beckett and James Joyce were friends and confidants. Although Joyce's writings have received more fame and publicity, Beckett won the Nobel Prize for Literature in 1969. His essays, short stories, novels, plays, and radio and television scripts are generally obscure and esoteric works addressing the absurdity and despair of life. His characters are typically engaged in meaningless habits to occupy their time, but have no purpose or mission and accomplish nothing. As he spoke with unflinching honesty about the emptiness of life, depicting people who have the freedom to choose but without a purpose or base of moral authority, he may well have been describing the modern-day worker, who toils in an environment of accelerated change and choice but with no purpose or meaning for his or her work.

The process of seeking understanding and application of our objectives at all levels of the organization was a never-ending task. It involved matters of the heart as well as the head, and it was not susceptible to standard management techniques of implementation. While at times the process was discouraging, it was also energizing as we realized the continuing potential for creativity, innovation, and growth as the result of a focus on the development of the whole person, not just a pair of hands to get the work done.

We found that, regardless of the task, people could find a sense of purpose and meaning in their work. They could develop a strong ethic that extended to care for others, a sense of community, and a willingness to give back and practice charity. Yes, they could develop a respect for the dignity and worth of their fellow workers and a willingness to serve as they had an opportunity to lead.

As they did so, they would honor their Creator, even though they may not have recognized Him as such. The community of work so developed could provide fertile ground for raising the question of God for good discussion and for an understanding of His redeeming love in one's life.

But is the ServiceMaster model just a rare exception in the way business is done or how a work environment is developed? Is the ServiceMaster model dependent upon its objectives or mission statement, or is it the people leading and managing the business that make the difference? Is the model working today as it did ten or fifteen years ago? What if I don't work in an environment like ServiceMaster? Is my work a calling or a curse?

The Virtue of Work

Over the last several years, we have seen a collapse in our financial markets, a domestic and global economic meltdown, foreclosures and unemployment at record levels, and a largely ineffective government attempt to correct the situation. While there are signs of improvement in our economy, there is still uncertainty about sustainability and the stability of our markets.

What were the causes of this financial collapse? Was it the self-interest of the profit-seekers compounded by unrestrained greed? Did it reflect the lack of a moral compass or the lack of care in the underwriting, packaging, and selling of innovative securities? Or are we to conclude that the up-and-down cycles of a market-driven economy are inevitable, as described in Joseph Schumpeter's term "creative destruction"?

President Obama, in reviewing what had occurred, suggested, "We have arrived at this point as a result of an era of profound irresponsibility that engulfed both private business firms and public institutions, including some of our largest corporations and seats of power in Washington, D.C."

Have we lost the desire to act responsibly as we do our work, as we lead and do business, and as we determine what is right for the common good? Will more legislation and regulation solve the problem? As we conduct business in a pluralistic society, can we agree on a source of moral authority? Can the business firm make money, create wealth, and also be a moral community for the development of human character and social concern? Can leadership make a difference? For those of us who are Christians and serving in the marketplace, does our faith have a relevance to the way we conduct business? Can the work of doing business be considered a ministry and, yes, even a calling of God? Can we affirm our faith in our work but not impose it?

As we try to answer these questions, we should first recognize reality—it is people who make markets work, people who can be right or wrong, good or evil, honest or dishonest, prudent or selfish. People are imperfect, weak sinners, and yet made in God's image with dignity and worth. People have been created with a freedom of choice but also should be morally responsible for their decisions and actions. We also should recognize that in dynamic and changing markets, the ethical and moral judgments required of business leaders cannot be determined solely by a set of rules. Neither can a socially or commercially desired result always be achieved by the interjection of more government funds or controls.

While legislative actions may bring a higher standard of accountability and provide more penalties for violations, they cannot assure the honesty, character, or integrity of the people involved. So how can these virtues become a more integral part of the way we work and do business? I would suggest that we need a transformation in how business firms are led and how future business leaders are taught. Those of us in the market who are followers of Jesus Christ should provide an example for others to follow. We need to bring our faith to work on Monday and learn to integrate the claims of our faith with the demands of our work.

In so doing, we should be concerned not only about what people do and how they do it in their work, but also about who people are becoming in the process. This important concept relating to the responsibility and accountability of the leader became a reality for me in my ServiceMaster career. During that time, I not only had the advantage of being mentored by my predecessors, but I also learned from the writings, friendship, and advice of Peter Drucker.

Drucker reminded us that in the business firm, or in any organization for that matter, we are not managing things, we are managing people, and the management of people is a liberal art that requires an understanding of the human condition. This includes the recognition that our humanity cannot be defined solely by its physical or rational nature, but also has a spiritual dimension. It is the spiritual dimension of our humanity that influences our character and our ability to determine right and wrong, to recognize good and evil, and to make moral judgments. It is the driver for developing a philosophy of life and a worldview that provides a moral standard that is not relative, that is other-oriented, and that functions even when there are no prescribed rules. Management as a liberal art is about treating people as the subject of work, not just the object of work. For the leader, it's about assuming the responsibility for crafting a culture of character and recognizing that the business firm has a duty of care not only to the customers it serves but also to the societies within which it operates.

To be effective and responsible in so doing, Drucker concluded that leaders must be able to draw upon the knowledge and insights of the humanities and social sciences, including psychology, philosophy, economics, history, and ethics. But he also said that because of the spiritual dimension of our humanity, there is a role of faith in determining the ultimate purpose and meaning for life and the work of the individual. As I mentioned in the first chapter, Joe Maciariello and Karen Linkletter have fully explored Drucker's concept of management as a liberal art in their book *Drucker's Lost Art of Management*.

Thus, in learning and understanding what it means to lead and manage people in a work environment, we need not be divorced from questions of faith or the role of God in our lives. For some in the secular academy or in the business world, this conclusion may be difficult to accept. I believe, however, that the work environment need not be emasculated to a neutrality of no belief. A belief that God exists and is at work in this world is not some relic of the past or, as Stephen Carter notes in his book *The Culture of Disbelief*, "like building model airplanes, just another hobby: something quiet, something private, something trivial—and not really a fit activity for intelligent, public-spirited adults."

The Calling of Work

As we consider this question of work—yes, even work in the marketplace—as a calling, where is the teaching of the church on this subject? David Miller, a graduate of Princeton Seminary who now leads a center at Princeton dedicated to faith and work, has done a great deal of research on this subject. In his book *God at Work*, he has concluded that, for the most part, the church has been silent on this subject and, in general, non-responsive to what he has identified as a growing interest among Christians to integrate the claims of their faith with the demands of their work.

Here is a letter I received from a graduate of a Christian college. It reflects some common misunderstandings of how God works and calls one to a purposeful life. The former student writes:

> I am very happy to report that, by God's grace and fullness, I actually did graduate. For the first time since age five, I am not a student.
>
> It's been a good four years of learning. I was an English major and a Bible minor. I can now read in the Greek New Testament. I know phrases like: inaugurated eschatology and hermeneutical fallacy. My interpretation of scripture has increased in both caution and confidence.
>
> I have made wonderful friends here, in breakfast Bible studies and noon prayer sessions for missions, in afternoons in the fall playing football and in the spring playing baseball, and late nights in the dorm having fun. The farewells will be very difficult.
>
> So, what's next? I am moving to Kansas City where I will be closer to my family. I'll find a job and pay off my student loans. What kind of a job? I really don't know—construction work or some type of administrative work for a business? I also will apply to various mission agencies. I feel called to the mission field and, in a year or two, I hope to be in full-time Christian service. Where, I don't know. Ethiopia? Papua New Guinea? India? I will wait for God's call to the right place.
>
> Please pray for me in the next couple of months. It is going to be quite a transition and, frankly, *I am not looking forward to it*. For the first time, I am leaving a Christian community to live among *ordinary, working Americans*. I am expecting a considerable

amount of uncertainty and loneliness, but I hope to develop some friends at the local church I will be attending.

What is this student saying? Could it be that his view is representative of a common understanding of "calling" within our church culture?

Is there some form of hierarchy in God's calling, with a special place for what people often refer to as "full-time Christian service?" Will we somehow miss out if we don't do something that fits into this category? Should we think of God's call in the context of a location or special place of service? Is it only about what we should do and the place where we should do it, or is it more about who we are and who we are becoming in our relationship with God? And by the way, where does ordinary work with those ordinary people fit in—the ordinary people whom God so loves and for whom Jesus died?

One of the best ways I found to respond to God's call to the marketplace and to lead in the development of the firm as a moral community was to seek to serve as I led—to reflect the principles that Jesus taught His disciples as He washed their feet, including the fact that no leader is greater than those being led. As I sought to serve, the truth of what I said could be measured by what I did. My faith and the ethic of my life became a reality as I was able to serve those I led. It was the salt and light of what I believed, and it provided a platform for me to share my faith. As we learn to invest ourselves in the lives of others, they will respond. God will provide opportunities for us to share, to speak the truth of our faith, to affirm our faith but not impose it.

Let me share two more experiences. They both involve ServiceMaster, but they need not be so limited. They deal with people's engagement with questions of faith in the work environment. Every one of us has the opportunity to so engage the people we work with.

As part of expanding our business to China, I made several trips there. After one of those trips, I received a note from a Chinese employee who had traveled with me as an interpreter and whom I had the opportunity to engage about questions of faith. Here's what Shu Zhang said:

> When I grew up in China, religions were forbidden and Mao's book became our bible. When I was five or six years old, I could recite Mao's quotations and even use them to judge and lecture the kids in the neighborhood.
>
> Mao said serve the people. Leaders should be public servants. This coincides with some of ServiceMaster's moral standard. When I think deeply, I see the difference that makes one work so successfully and the other collapse fatally. It must be the starting point of ServiceMaster to honor God and that every individual has been created in His image with dignity and worth.
>
> ServiceMaster is designed to be a big, tall tree with strong roots which penetrate extensively to almost every corner of a person's life. It is still growing in mine and I am still learning.

Shu is a thinking person. She felt accepted and respected in her work environment. She was confronted with life choices that went beyond doing a job and earning a living—choices about who she was becoming and how she could relate to God. She was growing and developing an understanding of herself and the purpose and meaning for her life.

The other experience involves James Smith. For several years before joining ServiceMaster, he was a homeless person, walking the streets of Chicago, consuming alcohol, and taking drugs when he could get them. He eventually ended up in a mission, desperate and wanting to take his life.

After a period of care and support in the mission, James wanted a job. ServiceMaster had a relationship with this mission and a program for helping people who were on welfare or otherwise disadvantaged to get back to work. James fit this program, so he came to work with us in an entry-level cleaning position, serving with other team members in providing housekeeping and janitorial services for one of our customers. James grew in his work. His boss invested in his development as a worker and also in the person he was becoming.

The time came when James was ready to be promoted to a supervisor. As part of his promotion, he came to our headquarters for a special training program. During one of his lunch hours, I had an opportunity to talk with James about his experiences on the street, coming to ServiceMaster, and how he viewed his job. His concluding remarks confirmed that something was happening in his life and in the person he was becoming: "My boss Jim cared about me and I have learned something about God and about servant leadership as I have come to ServiceMaster. You know, I have been helped so much that I just want to give it back in whatever job I have."

Channel of Faith

For me, the world of business has become a channel of distribution for fulfilling and living my faith—a channel that has reached from a janitor's closet in Saudi Arabia to the Great Hall of the People in Beijing, from sweeping streets in Osaka, Japan, to ringing the bell on the New York Stock Exchange. The marketplace has provided a wonderful opportunity for me to embrace and engage those who do not believe the way I do, but whom God loves and who should see by my words and actions the reality of His love.

Can Christian values make a difference in the way a business is led, the way a person performs his or her responsibilities? You bet they can. Creating cultures of character requires leaders to know what they believe and why they believe it, to seek truth and know their source of moral authority, and to know what is right even when there is no code of conduct. The global marketplace provides a wonderful opportunity for followers of Jesus Christ to live and share their faith. There is a common language of performance in the market that crosses secular, cultural, and religious barriers. When there is performance, people listen, and, yes, as some people listen, they respond to the redemptive message of God's love.

ServiceMaster was a channel of faith for sharing and living my faith that stretched from Saudi Arabia to the Great Hall of the People in China.

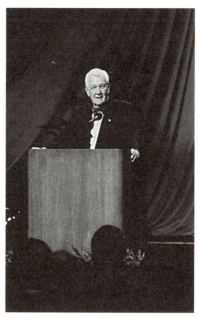

As Joshua came to the closing days of his leadership of the nation of Israel, he challenged the people to fear God and faithfully serve Him. It was a challenge, not a command, for God does not compel anyone to follow or worship Him. In Joshua's conclusion, he emphasized this point when he said: "But if serving the LORD seems undesirable to you, then choose for yourselves this day whom you will serve. . . . But as for me and my household, we will serve the LORD" (Joshua 24:15, NIV).

The Hebrew word translated "serve" is *avodah*, and it can also mean "worship" or "work." Yes, that's right, our work, whatever it is, can also be worship to the God we love as we serve and live out our faith. Our workplaces can become centers of worship as we bring alive the reality that Jesus lived and died so that those He created and loved may know Him as God and Savior.

As Christians, God has called each of us to be in the world but not part of it (John 15:19). He has called us to be excellent in what we do, whether we call it a job, a profession, or a ministry. And when we excel in what we do, whatever that may be, as a lawyer, businessperson, minister, or educator, and live our faith in a way that cannot be ignored or contained, we have the platform to share and engage others with our faith. The choice is ours. Who will we serve this day and tomorrow? Will we be vehicles for use by God to help people find a truth that is worth seeking and has eternal value?

Remember, you can buy a person's time, you can buy a person's physical presence at a given place, you can even buy a measured amount of skilled muscular motions for an eight-hour day, but you cannot buy enthusiasm, you cannot buy initiative, and you cannot buy loyalty or commitment. Neither can you buy the devotion of the hearts, minds, and souls of the people. When you can align a person's mission in life with the mission and work of the firm, there will be enthusiasm, initiative, loyalty, and devotion. You will be building a community. Your work will be a calling. You will be integrating the claims of your faith with the demands of your work.

Former British Prime Minister Margaret Thatcher, in a speech to the general assembly of the Church of Scotland, said, "There is little hope for democracy if the hearts of men and women in democratic societies cannot be touched by a call to something greater than themselves."

I conclude with these lines from T. S. Eliot's "Choruses from 'The Rock'":

> When the Stranger says: "What is the meaning of this city?
> Do you huddle close together because you love each other?"
> What will you answer? "We all dwell together,
> To make money from each other"? or "This is a community"?
> . . .
> Oh my soul be prepared for the coming of the Stranger.
> Be prepared for him who knows how to ask questions.

Is our work a calling or a curse? How are we preparing people for the coming of the Stranger—the One Who knows how to ask questions, Who has called us to have a relationship with Him, and Who desires us to honor Him in our work?

4

Forks in the Road

*Choices to be made that may
include a way less traveled*

Two roads diverged in a yellow wood,
And sorry I could not travel both
And be one traveler, long I stood
And looked down one as far as I could
To where it bent in the undergrowth;

Then took the other, as just as fair,
And having perhaps the better claim
Because it was grassy and wanted wear;
Though as for that the passing there
Had worn them really about the same,

And both that morning equally lay
In leaves no step had trodden black.
Oh, I kept the first for another day!
Yet knowing how way leads on to way
I doubted if I should ever come back.

I shall be telling this with a sigh
Somewhere ages and ages hence:
Two roads diverged in a wood, and I—
I took the one less traveled by,
And that has made all the difference.

ROBERT FROST

The winds and currents of life are always changing, requiring new tacks to be taken or involving choices between two different directions, one of which may be a new course that pushes us beyond our comfort zone. Often such choices involve significant unknowns, with the potential for upside but also with the risk of failure. How do we know at the time of the choice if one option is better than another? Or if, as the result of the choice we make, we will later sigh and wonder about what we might have missed on that "road not taken"? If we believe God has a plan for our lives, how can we know His way as we make these life-changing choices?

A Choice for a Lifetime

Some of the choices we make may have consequences that last a lifetime and involve a commitment to, and require a commitment from, others. Marriage is such a choice. By the time Judy and I got married, we had been dating for four years and thought we knew what marriage and living together were going to look like. But now, after fifty-five years of marriage, we agree that what has made it a great choice and a great marriage is not all we knew about each other before the choice was made, but what we did since the choice to mold our lives together.

This principle of "making a decision work" and building into that decision the reality and commitment of implementation is often more important in making a good choice than what we may know at the time the choice is made. Career choices are often like that. When we are in our early twenties, the question that often pops up is, "What are you going to do with the rest of your life?"

A Choice for a Career

When I reached the age of twenty-two, I had been married for almost a year and was looking forward to graduating from college. But I still did not know what I was going to do. As I look back at that time, I am thankful for a patient wife, a supportive father-in-law, and a college professor named Doc Volkman, a wise counselor who guided me to consider a career in the practice of law. His recommendation to his alma mater, Northwestern, helped me not only to get admitted but also to receive a full tuition scholarship.

For me, this was a confirming word from God to proceed even though I knew little about what law school or the practice of law would be like. I was unsure about how I was going to do two things at once: go to school and support a family that would soon include our first child.

Judy's dad put his trust in me before I could prove I was a provider and he continued to invest in our family until God took him Home.

Again, what made it a good choice was what was done after the choice was made. With the help and support of Judy; the assistance of her father in providing an apartment over his doctor's office; the love and support of my mother; and the continued growth of my house-painting business, which provided the financial resources for everyday living, we all worked together to make it happen. I was able to finish law school three years later in the top ten percent of my class and to secure a good job at a major law firm in Chicago.

I soon found that the practice of law had its own set of time demands. There was much for me to learn. The firm I joined represented some of the largest corporations and some of the wealthiest people in the Chicago area. My interests were in business and tax law. As I grew in my knowledge and understanding of the law, I found the practice of law stimulating, rewarding, and consuming. I also noticed that most of the successful partners of the firm were continuing to find the practice stimulating, rewarding, and consuming. The one major negative was that there seemed to be no letup on the time demands.

A friend of mine who had been in law school with me and who also had done his undergraduate work at Wheaton noticed the same thing occurring in the large firm where he worked. After four years of working in large firms, we both chose to leave and together we opened our own firm in Wheaton, a suburb of Chicago close to where we lived. We could shorten our commute by two and a half hours and have more time with our families. By now, we both had a client base, but we knew that the fees from that client base would barely cover our overhead.

Starting our own firm would be a struggle. We would have to borrow money to cover our first year or two of operations. We had little comprehension of the time it would take to grow the practice and to manage that growth.

Soon after the doors opened, the practice did begin to grow, and at the end of the first nine months we were able to begin paying back the loan. Finally I was able to cover the cost of groceries and my family was no longer eating food bought with borrowed money.

Within three years, we had the opportunity to merge with another firm, and by the end of the next year, the firm had grown to four of us as partners and five associates with a strong business and estate-planning client base and with one of the partners dedicated to litigation.

The practice of law continued to be stimulating and rewarding, but it was even more consuming. Somewhere in the process, the extra time with family had vanished.

One of my clients was a large, family-owned, multistate garbage and refuse company. At the time, the industry was consolidating, and my client was considering either going public or merging with a company in Texas that had already gone public. I soon found myself engaged in the merger discussions and then representing my client in negotiating the merger with the Texas company. The process involved three months of extensive legal work by our firm and by another firm we hired that specialized in antitrust law.

This added work, in addition to my regular practice, was definitely stimulating and rewarding, but also very, very consuming.

Two weeks after the deal closed, my wife found me unconscious on the bathroom floor. She was able to awaken me and then called her father, who called an ambulance to take me to the hospital. The doctors at the hospital found that I had a very low blood count and, based on my medical history, suspected that my ulcer was hemorrhaging. After a few more tests, they confirmed their initial diagnosis and said I would need surgery. The surgery was a success, but I had some complications with my recovery and my hospital stay lasted three weeks.

I had a lot of time to think and pray during that period. I had achieved success in the practice of law, but had I worked as hard at becoming a good husband to Judy and a good father for my children? Was God trying to tell me something through this illness about the way I was living?

Time for Change and a Step of Faith

Wheaton College was one of my clients, and the president of the college, Dr. Hudson Armerding, was a regular visitor during my hospital stay. I respected him for his leadership ability, his academic knowledge, and his spiritual insight. He was a great comfort during those trying days of recovery and seeking to understand what God might be saying to me.

On the day before I was discharged from the hospital, Hudson came for a visit. He told me he had been praying for me and felt I should consider leaving the practice of law and coming to work with him at Wheaton College. He needed someone my age to head up the leadership and management of the college's business affairs and advance its fundraising efforts. He also suggested that the Business and Economics Department would like me to teach some other courses in addition to the business law class I had been teaching as an adjunct professor. I was surprised by his offer, and my initial response was that I did not have the skills or experience to do what he wanted me to do. I felt that my focus should be on getting back to work at the law firm as soon as possible.

During the weeks that followed, as Judy and I talked and prayed about what Dr. Armerding had offered, she began encouraging me to explore the opportunity. I knew the salary that the college could pay me would be substantially less than what I was earning in the law firm, but was money the issue? I knew there would be enough to support my family and, if it was the right thing to do, God would provide.

The next week, I talked to my law partners about the opportunity and discussed how we would handle my clients if I were to leave and go to the college. They were very gracious and agreed to give me a leave of absence if I decided to go. If it didn't work out, I could always come back to a partnership role in the firm.

God seemed to be pushing me through this open door, but could I do the job? Why would God want a lawyer to try to do the job of a senior college administrator? It didn't make much sense to me. If I took the job, I would definitely be choosing a road less traveled.

I knew I could work with and learn from Hudson, but I was

unsure about whether I could work with the trustee who was chairman of the Finance Committee of the board. This was a key board committee and the one that would be reviewing the areas under my leadership. The chairman's name was Ken Hansen. He was also chairman of a company called ServiceMaster. I had heard that he was a sharp, tough, no-nonsense businessman.

More than a month after my discharge from the hospital, Hudson called and asked me to lunch. As we ate together, he pressed me again for a decision about coming to the college. I told him of my talk with Judy and with the partners of my firm. Then I explained my reservation about being able to work with Ken. Hudson assured me that although Ken was strong and direct, he was also fair, had a good heart, and was always seeking the best for the college. As we finished our lunch, he asked me to please make a decision within the next week before the upcoming board meeting.

Soon after I returned to my office, I received a call. I heard the voice at the other end say: "Hello. This is Ken Hansen. When do you go home from work today?" I replied, "About 5:30 or 6 o'clock." Ken then said, "Could you meet me in President Armerding's office at 6:15?" I said sure. Then Ken hung up.

At the appointed time, I arrived at the president's office to meet with Hudson and Ken. After shaking hands and greeting each other, we sat down and Ken thrust a piece of paper toward me with the words, "Will this satisfy you?" As I read what he had written on the paper, I was shocked. It was his resignation as a trustee of Wheaton College.

My immediate response was that such an action was not necessary. There then followed a very open and productive discussion about the way he worked and the way I worked, and also about my reservations concerning whether I had the skills and background to do the job I was being asked to do. The meeting ended with me choosing to take the job. As we were about to leave, Ken looked at me and said, "Bill, I can't change the way I am, but if I ever get in your way, you have to kick me in the shins."

Little did Ken or I realize on that day how closely we would work together in the future—not only at the college, but later at ServiceMaster. Although there were times when I felt like kicking him, they always turned out to be important times of learning.

There was always something to learn from Ken, and he was a teacher who was always willing to listen and learn from the person he was seeking to teach. He never dealt for his own interest. He was always willing to step aside from a position he held or from a point he was trying to make if doing so would be in the best interest of the organization he was serving. There was a choice to be made that day in Hudson's office, and he knew how to bring it to issue and closure.

But for it to be a good choice, it still had to be implemented, which for the most part would be up to me—with God's help and guidance.

The practice of law had become a jealous mistress in my life. If I had continued down that road, I might have lost my marriage and my family. God allowed an illness to stop me in my tracks. I had reached a fork in the road and needed to take another path. As I started down this new path, I had doubts about whether I could measure up and do the job. There was that lingering question of why a lawyer was needed for a job like this.

The answer to that question, in what I believe was a confirmation from God, came six months later, when the college was named as one of two beneficiaries of a charitable trust created under the will of a friend of the college who had recently passed away. The assets of the trust consisted of two operating coal companies—one in Pennsylvania and the other in West Virginia.

There were many legal issues involved in the estate and in the way the trust was established. The named trustees were also the directors and officers of the coal companies, so they had a decided conflict of interest. They had control over their own jobs and salaries. Soon after the trusts were established, they approved salary increases that more than tripled their incomes. There were also inadequate provisions in the estate for the surviving spouse and questions regarding the tax qualification and administration of the trust.

In addition to these legal and tax issues, an oil embargo had recently been imposed, affecting the United States and resulting in an increase in the price of oil and coal. The price of coal went from $10 a ton to $100 a ton. Based on the coal reserves held by these companies, the combined value of the trust increased to more than $40 million.

It was clearly in the best interest of the two beneficiaries of the charitable trust to sell the companies. However, it was in the best interest of the trustees if the companies were not sold and their jobs remained secure, with them controlling what they would be paid.

The legal, tax, and people issues involved in seeking an orderly and fair sale and in distributing the assets of this estate became a big part of my job at Wheaton. It took more than four years and many trips to Pittsburgh before the companies were sold and the proceeds distributed. It became one of the largest single-endowment gifts the college had ever received. God had a purpose for the use of my legal talents and background, and, in the process, God also taught me many lessons about working, managing people, and accomplishing organizational objectives.

After the legal issues in the estate were resolved, the coal companies had been sold, and I had recruited two new leaders for the areas reporting to me, I felt my time at Wheaton was over. I had learned a lot about life and the way it should be lived from Hudson and my other colleagues at the college, and I felt I could return to the practice of law without it becoming a jealous mistress.

A Way Less Traveled

It was then that I was recruited, at the age of thirty-seven, to consider taking another road that would involve a leadership position at ServiceMaster. The story of my choice to go to ServiceMaster has already been told in chapter 3. One of the major lessons I learned at Wheaton was that if you earnestly seek God's way in life and doors begin to open, you should walk through them, even if at the time of the choice there are still some substantial unknowns. God's confirming voice often comes after you have taken that first step of faith.

The reality of life is that there will always be forks in the road. The world around us is a moving target. Tomorrow will be different from today and change often requires choices to be made even on what may appear to be a road less traveled.

While we may think of our choices as personal or individual, they often involve the lives of others. This is especially true when we are in leadership positions and have responsibilities for the growth and development of the people who are following our lead.

C. WILLIAM POLLARD AND KENNETH T. WESSNER
SERVICEMASTER

■ *When their core business of hospital housekeeping weakened, President Pollard, 51 (left), and Chairman Wessner, 67, converted ServiceMaster to a partnership, borrowed, diversified, and kept it Star No. 1.*

ServiceMaster as a partnership was a road less traveled with high risk and a potential for great benefits. (From *Fortune* magazine, June 5, 1989 © 1989 Time Inc. Used under license. Photo by Katherine Lambert. Used with permission.)

A choice for a way less traveled may have more risk and be more difficult to understand, but also, in its risks and difficulties, it may provide more opportunities and benefits for those taking the journey. I was faced with such a choice in my third year as CEO of ServiceMaster. We had reached our objective of becoming a $1 billion company and had set our sights on reaching $2 billion within the next four years. To do so, however, would require some choices and changes. While our two business units—the franchise business and the management services business—were healthy and growing, we needed to add a third growth curve if we were going to achieve our objective. In the planning process, we had concluded that the growing number of two-wage-earner homes provided a demand factor for providing more services to homeowners, and that providing these services to this market could become our third growth curve. (I will talk more about the planning process we went through to reach that decision in chapter 7.)

We also, however, needed to develop a different structure for our business operations to provide a more efficient use of our growing cash flow. There were several options for a change in our structure, and, with the help of Goldman Sachs, we decided to choose a road less traveled and convert our public corporation to a public limited partnership. For the company and our shareholders, it would mean there would be only one tax to pay, and as a result we would be able to increase our cash reserves for developing our third growth curve and at the same time increase dividend payments to our shareholders.

The process of liquidating a public corporation and simultaneously forming a public partnership was complicated and required the approval of both our shareholders and the U.S. Securities and Exchange Commission. We would be one of only a few public partnerships listed on the New York Stock Exchange. There was also an open question about whether mutual funds could hold partnership units as a permitted asset and whether the profit-sharing plan for our employees could hold partnership units. Also, as part of the liquidation, some of our individual shareholders would have a tax to pay.

We were advised by our attorneys that in order to get a favorable tax opinion on the transaction, several individuals would have to serve as individual general partners along with a corporate general partner, with the attendant personal liability for the acts of the company this would entail. As CEO, I was responsible for initiating the choice to move in this direction; therefore, I believed I should be the first to serve as an individual general partner and put my personal assets at risk. After I did, three other senior officers agreed to do likewise. I will always be thankful and appreciative of their willingness to do so.

There was also the added risk of completing this change and conversion within a three-month period. It had to be done before the year ended because a change in the tax law regarding corporate liquidations would become effective the next year, and this would adversely affect the transaction.

We made the choice to move forward. However, once again I felt very inadequate for the task before me. It was a choice I had prayed much about, asking God's guidance and direction. It could be beneficial to thousands and thousands of people or it could be a failure in its execution, with a corresponding disruption and cost to those same people.

There were rough waters and unpredictable currents to navigate during the next few months. Within weeks, we were also presented with the opportunity to acquire Terminix. This would provide a major new thrust for the company for our third growth curve, which would later become known as our consumer services business. It would be the first big acquisition for ServiceMaster, and it meant we would have to borrow more than $165 million. This acquisition also had to be closed by the end of the year. Could we do two things at once? Terminix had other potential buyers, so we had to win against competition and sell ourselves to the seller and senior management of Terminix if we were to be successful in buying the company.

Carlos Cantu, Chuck Stair, and Bob Erickson were a team of leaders who would walk and sometimes run with me on this way less traveled as we built the firm for the future. (ServiceMaster photo. Used with permission.)

No sooner had we decided to move forward on both fronts than we also were presented with the opportunity to acquire another company that would give us the capability of providing food management services to the educational market. This acquisition also had to be closed before the year's end.

Two sets of law firms had to be managed. Many accounting and tax issues had to be resolved. We had to develop new banking relationships to secure the funding for these acquisitions. Then there was a negative sell-off of our stock just before our shareholders meeting, in which we were seeking approval for the transaction. But as a confirming positive, it was publicly announced that Warren Buffett had just become a major new shareholder of ServiceMaster. In addition to all that was going on with the conversion and acquisitions, we still had a business to run and another year to close out with growth in revenue and earnings.

Our plan for the reorganization and the acquisitions was approved and completed by December 30, with one day to spare. Many people worked hard and skillfully to accomplish this result. I will always be thankful for their efforts. It was an extraordinary result that happened because of a choice to take a road less traveled; a choice that had to be successfully implemented in order to have a positive result; a choice that presented challenges I had never faced before. A sustaining force for me during this time of tension and decision-making was the comfort that God was there, walking beside me and providing confirmations along the way.

When we pray for direction and God's way, I have found that He does not play hide and seek with us. He either gives us that sense of direction to move forward or He does not. There will be times of doubt, but if His hand is in it, there will also be times of confirmation. In some cases, the result will not be what we expected or even, at first, what we wanted. At times, there will be loss or failure, with important lessons to be learned. It is important to remember that God always measures results with eternity in view.

Choosing with Eternity in View

Earlier I mentioned my first mentoring and learning session with Ken Hansen. As I close this chapter with the thought of measuring life choices with eternity in view, I want to share about my last mentoring and learning session with Ken.

Ken's wife, Jean, had passed away and he was living alone in a retirement community in Southern California. He had recently been diagnosed with terminal cancer. I wanted to visit him in person, so I traveled to California to see him and arrived at his home at 11 o'clock in the morning.

When I knocked on his door, he opened it and greeted me in his pajamas. I offered my apology if I had awakened him and he promptly reminded me I should have remembered that he was up early that morning as was his custom, having his personal devotions and prayer time with God. My next question was why he still had on his pajamas and why I was still standing on the doorstep. His response was quick: "Bill, follow me and I will show you why I am still wearing my pajamas."

I followed him into his bedroom. He opened his closet door and said: "I have made a choice, Bill. All my clothes are gone. I have given them away. I don't need them anymore. I know where I am going. While I wait to go, I will stay here, pray and visit with my family, pray for the missionaries I support, and pray for you and all my friends at ServiceMaster. Bill, I have been everywhere I wanted to go in this world and now I just want to go Home." We then went into the living room and talked about ServiceMaster, and we closed our visit with a time of prayer.

Ken, dressed in his pajamas, was reminding me of the most important choice we can make in life: to accept the offer of God's redeeming love. When we do so, the ultimate result will be measured with eternity in view. It is the great hope of our faith that as we leave this life we will be present with our Lord and Savior.

> For we know that if the tent that is our earthly home is destroyed, we have a building from God, a house not made with hands, eternal in the heavens. . . . We know that while we are at home in the body we are away from the Lord . . . and we would rather be away from the body and at home with the Lord. (2 Corinthians 5:1, 6, 8)

5

The Awesome Responsibility of Leadership

A leader has only one choice to make—to lead or mislead.

Peter Drucker's statement may be all that needs to be said to affirm the title of this chapter.

Leadership is needed at all levels of life: in our families, in our workplaces, in our governments, and in our churches and other places of worship. If the tides of life provide us an opportunity to lead others, will we assume the awesome responsibility to do so?

Leaders should know what they believe, why they believe it, and how that belief will benefit others. They must know where they are going and why it is important for people to follow. They must be able to respond to the changing currents of life. When there is misleadership or an absence of leadership, there will be detrimental results—a net loss to the people who are following. *There is no middle ground!*

Leadership Is Just a Means

As mentioned in previous chapters, Drucker was both a friend and an adviser during my years at ServiceMaster. There were often times when I sought his advice about a challenging leadership issue I was facing. The counsel I received always reflected his years of experience advising and working with leaders, his rich understanding of history, and his exhaustive reading and research on the subject.

Peter Drucker was a thought leader and became a wise adviser, mentor, and friend. (ServiceMaster photo. Used with permission.)

For Peter, leadership was not about the topics often emphasized in many of the popular books on leadership, including leadership qualities, personality traits, charisma, or lists of the seven or ten characteristics of a good leader. He believed the essence of leadership was performance, achieving meaningful results. He often pointed out that leadership, in and of itself, was not good or desirable. He would go on to say that leadership was just a "means," and that "to what end?" was the crucial question. For Drucker, and for me, the end goal of leadership involved the people who followed, the direction they were headed, and who they were becoming as they fulfilled the mission and purpose of the organization being led.

One of the first tasks of a leader is to determine whether the mission and purpose of the organization being led are meaningful. People work for a cause, not just a living. One of the reasons why Drucker was so interested in ServiceMaster was our mission, as incorporated in our four objectives: "To Honor God in All We Do; To Help People Develop; To Pursue Excellence; and To Grow Profitably." The first two objectives were "end goals" and the second two were "means goals."

Peter saw us as more than just a business firm making money by serving customers. We were a moral community held together by a commitment to a common purpose that extended beyond creating wealth for our shareholders. We were about developing the whole person who was producing the results of the firm, and we had the potential to make significant contributions to the societies within which we worked. The writers of the Harvard Case Studies on ServiceMaster saw the same potential when they discussed our people focus as being instrumental in breaking the cycle of failure among service workers.

In our business, we found that when there was an alignment between the mission of the firm and a person's reasons for being and doing, there was the potential for extraordinary results and for the growth and development of the people producing those results. For us, this was the essence of performance: a result we as leaders were responsible for achieving.

The Obligation to Those Who Follow

Our leadership was not just a duty or a function of title or rank; it was the fulfilling of our obligation to the people who followed. In his book *Leadership Jazz*, Max De Pree referred to this obligation as the leader's posture of indebtedness. As a leader implements this commitment, there develops a relationship and a bond of trust with the followers that confirm the leader's legitimacy, authority, and reliability.

One of the best ways I found to communicate this responsibility and obligation of leadership was to picture it as a debt, a liability, if you will, on the balance sheet of the leader.

When people were given the opportunity to assume significant leadership positions at ServiceMaster, we also gave them the opportunity to purchase some ServiceMaster stock. I remember a time when I was discussing this opportunity with one of our newly appointed officers. He had asked to see me because he was unsure whether he wanted to purchase more stock since he would have to borrow some money to do so. He was delighted about his new promotion and new responsibility to lead one of our divisions, but he was concerned about the risk he would be assuming if he incurred additional indebtedness.

As part of discussing this concern with him, I asked him to make a simple T account balance sheet of his assets and liabilities. When he did so and showed me his work sheet, I noticed he had listed only one liability on his balance sheet, and that was the mortgage on his house. I asked why he hadn't listed the obligation he was assuming to the eight hundred people in the division he was going to lead. I followed up with a series of other questions, including:

- In a year from now, will there be opportunities for one thousand people or six hundred people in this division?
- Will there be growth in customers served and in the revenue and profit of this division?
- Will there be the potential for increases in compensation for the people and opportunities for promotions within the division?
- How many people in this division are the principal breadwinners in their homes, with families dependent upon their paychecks?

- How many will be better people, better spouses, better parents, better leaders in their communities because of their growth and development in their work in this division?
- Will your leadership have anything to do with the answers to these questions? If it does, you are assuming an obligation that is a much bigger debt than any amount you would have to borrow to purchase more stock. If your leadership doesn't have anything to do with the answers to these questions, then you are telling me we don't need a leader in this division.

After considering these questions, he asked for more time—not only to think about whether he would buy the stock, but also about whether he wanted to take on the obligation of the new assignment. For me, this was a positive sign. He was beginning to realize the awesome responsibility of leadership and the obligation he would be assuming to the people who would follow. A few days later, he called me and said he was ready to assume the obligation of leadership and that he would buy the stock.

A year later, he was making a big difference in the lives of the people he was leading and in the performance of this division. He was not only fulfilling the obligation he had assumed, but was learning how to serve those he was leading and to subordinate his desires to the needs and development of the people who were following.

The Opportunity to Serve

This dimension of serving is often referred to as servant leadership. There are many books on this subject, and I have discussed it in several chapters of the books I have already written.

It is not a new subject. It has roots in the teachings of Jesus. The often-cited example is His teaching on the night He was betrayed. It was His last time with His disciples before He was crucified. As He took a towel and a basin of water and then washed their feet, He reminded them that their roles would be changing in the future. They would no longer be disciples. They would become leaders in spreading the word of God's redeeming love and in building His church. He was teaching them in a very practical and poignant way that effective leadership in His church would not be about them—the titles, positions of authority, or platforms they would assume. Instead, it would be about the people who followed and the nurturing and growth of these people in their faith to the point where they would be able to multiply themselves in the lives of others.

Does this example fit in today's world? There is certainly no scarcity of feet to wash, and towels are always available. I suggest that the only limitation, if there is one, is the ability of leaders to exercise the spirit of humility, subordinate self, and become engaged with compassion and love for those they lead. When we lead by serving, we assume a commitment to be examples in our public and private lives, to be initiators of change and growth, and to be always willing to do whatever we ask others to do.

Servant leadership has always been a learning experience for me. Unfortunately, there are often many trappings around leadership positions, including the perks and prestige of office and the arrogance of success that tempts leaders to focus on themselves and think they have all the answers rather than to focus on their responsibility to others. It is the evil of hubris. It is often subtle and can have a cumulative effect on judgment unless it is nipped in the bud.

The Evil of Hubris

An example from my experience may help to illustrate this point. One of the benefits of my friendship with Peter Drucker was that he never hesitated to point out areas where I could improve my leadership. One of those important moments of learning occurred when we were traveling together to conduct a management seminar in Tokyo.

After the seminar was over, Peter and I had dinner together. I shared my disappointment and, yes, even anger that no one from the leadership team of our Japanese business partner had come to the seminar. They had been invited and had promised to attend. Since some of our current and prospective customers had been there, it had been an opportunity for the leaders of our Japanese partner to learn and also to make important business connections.

I explained to Peter that we had recently decided to delay bringing one of our new service lines to Japan and that our partners were no doubt upset with the decision, and this was probably the reason they had not come. I also told Peter I had decided to cancel my planned trip the next day to their headquarters in Osaka, and instead I would take an early flight back to the United States. He encouraged me to rethink my position and gave some advice based on his understanding of Japanese culture. Although I politely listened, I had made up my mind I was not going to accept his advice and that I would reschedule my flight the next morning.

After dinner, we returned to our respective hotel rooms. At about 10:30, Peter called and asked if I would come to his room. He was still concerned about my reactions and wanted a further discussion.

As Peter opened the door, I could tell by the look on his face that he was troubled. He told me to sit on the chair near his bed and he sat down on the edge of his bed. He looked me straight in the eye and said: "Bill, you are suffering from hubris. It's time for you to eat some humble pie." He explained how quickly leaders can lose touch with the reality of their responsibility and be consumed by pride and self. He pointed out that my job as a leader was to go to Osaka, meet with our business partners, resolve our differences, and rebuild the relationship. This result was needed for the continued growth of our business in Japan and for the opportunities it would provide to our people. It was my job as a leader to do this; it was not something I could delegate.

It was great advice. The next morning, I was on the train to Osaka. My meeting with the president of our business partner and his team accomplished the right result for our business and for our people as we renewed our relationship. The lesson was clear: my leadership responsibility was not about me or my feelings. It was about what should be done for our business and for our people.

There is another chapter to this story. Six months after this meeting, the president of our business partner in Japan died suddenly. Soon after I heard the news, his wife contacted me and asked if I would come to Japan and participate as a special friend in his funeral ceremony. I was honored, but frankly, I was somewhat perplexed about how I could do so in a way that would reflect the sincerity of our friendship while also sharing the great hope of my faith and the truth of God's redeeming love. I knew it would be a traditional Japanese ceremony led by both a Buddhist monk and a Shinto priest, and I did not want my words to disrupt or offend.

At the funeral, I shared some of what we had discussed the last time we had met, including the importance of forgiveness in building relationships of trust. I closed with a word about what God's forgiveness meant in my life and about His offer of forgiveness for all who would receive it. My message was well received. Once again, God in His wisdom used the doing of business to cross the lines of culture and faith to honor the truth of His Word.

As a leader seeks to be an example for others to follow, it is important to remember that actions speak louder than words. If I had not made that trip to Osaka and eaten some humble pie, there would have been no opportunity and no words to speak six months later.

Acknowledging Mistakes, Seeking Forgiveness

Mistakes in leading people are often painful. Implicit in leadership are the power and authority to make decisions that affect others. You can be right in your intent and decision but wrong in how you use power to implement that decision. The mistakes I have made as a leader that hurt the most are ones that resulted in breached relationships. Sometimes, in seeking to achieve specific performance goals, I have pressed too hard for results without understanding the subjective factors of fear, insecurity, or risk influencing a person's substandard performance. The pain of honestly facing mistakes and seeking forgiveness is part of the learning process of leading and serving others. They often result in a greater relationship of trust with those you lead. This is part of learning the awesome responsibility of leadership.

However, if a leader's mistake or failure results in a breach of trust, forgiveness does not necessarily mean the former relationship of trust has been restored. An act of distrust is not easily forgotten. For trust to be restored, it has to be re-earned, and that takes time. Without trust, leadership is not effective. If trust is not restored, the leader needs to be removed; otherwise, there is the risk of the leader becoming a tyrant as part of getting things done.

There were times when I had to remove leaders and times when I had to terminate their employment. For me, it was always a painful decision. There were questions about whether I had done everything I could have to support and develop that person. Was the original appointment a bad fit? Did the person have the skills and knowledge to do the assigned job? Was it more my fault than the person's fault that he or she had failed?

A decision to terminate is more often than not a mixed bag; seldom is there a clear-cut case of fault. Yet a decision has to be made. When there is ineffective leadership, the people who follow suffer. A decision delayed results in the "stealing" of their opportunities to perform and flourish in their growth and development.

Knowing Right and Wrong

It is important for leaders to exemplify in word and deed the difference between right and wrong, and that their speech and actions reflect an ethic that can be trusted.

When I retired from my leadership role at ServiceMaster, we were managing and employing more than two hundred thousand people, delivering services to more than ten million customers in the United States and in forty-five other countries. There was a wide diversity among our people—diversity of skills, talents, gender, race, ethnicity, cultural backgrounds, and religious beliefs. What are the common rights and wrongs with such a mix of people?

As we developed certain standards for the ethical behavior of our people, our core value system was centered on our view of the dignity, worth, and potential of every person regardless of the differences cited above. It was wrong to deceive or withhold material information from our people. It was right to have a compensation system that represented a fair distribution of the results of the firm and provided every employee with the opportunity for ownership in the firm.

We believed the truth of what we said should be told by what we did. We believed that, to our customers, truth involved exceeding their expectations in the quality of the services we delivered. We all shared in the risk of the performance of the firm, with those in senior management assuming higher risk. We were all to take part in developing the whole person, not only in what they were doing in their jobs but also in the people they were becoming.

We sought to be an open community. This principle was reflected in the way we designed our corporate headquarters. Nobody worked behind closed doors. Glass was everywhere, confirming our desire to have an open office and an open mind. No executive office captured an outside window; the view to the outside was available to all.

We made our share of mistakes in implementing these ethical standards, but our first objective was a constant reminder that the rights and wrongs relating to the treatment of people should never be compromised. This objective required both fairness and accountability. Our mission became the organizing principle for the firm wherever we operated. It was a self-correcting tool. When we made mistakes or acted in a way inconsistent with our mission, the mistakes were typically flushed out into the open for correction and forgiveness.

Noel Tichy, a professor at the University of Michigan's Graduate School of Business, in his book *The Leadership Engine*, describes companies that build and develop leaders at every level of the organization. One of the companies he studied and reported on was ServiceMaster. At first, he was concerned about whether we would be a valid example because of our mission and objectives. He writes:

> For many people who don't know the folks at ServiceMaster, the stated value of "To honor God in all we do" is troubling. Before we went to visit them, one of my colleagues suggested that their religious orientation might make them unsuitable as models for more "normal" organizations. But the truth is that . . . when you get to know the people at ServiceMaster, you quickly see there are no traces of ethereal other-worldliness about them. They are serious businesspeople firmly focused on winning. In Pollard's recent book, *The Soul of the Firm*, he talks about the link between God and profits. "Profit is a means in God's world to be used and invested, not an end to be worshipped. Profit . . . is a standard for determining the effectiveness of our combined efforts."

Tichy goes on to say:

> ServiceMaster has achieved such adherence to its values . . . because everyone from [the top] on down works at making them an everyday reality. One of [their] twenty-one leadership principles says (No. 6), "If you don't live it, you don't believe it." And they really mean it. Service permeates all the way to the highest level of the company. . . . And no matter how senior they become, each spends at least one day a year performing front-line service.

How one determines right and wrong and how one exercises authority in the appointment or termination of a person's job are two of the most important questions that need to be asked in determining whether a person has the integrity to lead. If leaders have no ultimate reference point for determining what is morally right or wrong, or if they fail to accept their potential responsibility in the nonperformance of those they lead, they don't understand the meaning of integrity.

Defining Reality

The essence of performance is achieving meaningful results. It has been my experience that in order to achieve meaningful results, leaders must be able to define reality. They must know what is happening to the business at the margin, understand the trends of today that will impact tomorrow, and initiate needed changes for continued growth.

One of the challenges for leaders, as the organizations or units they lead grow in size and complexity, is that most of the reports they receive on whether the desired results are being achieved deal with averages, which relate more to the past than the present and are often not indicative of future trends.

An example of a business measurement that is indicative of what may happen in the future is a marginal revenue/marginal cost curve that provides a view of the returns from adding new business. This information helps leaders understand whether trends are developing that indicate future growth or reduction in the profitability of the firm. The world is always changing and moving. Tides are coming in or going out. Good businesses always collect more competitors, which often can change the rules of the ball game. Employee turnover rates, customer retention rates, and sales close ratios are also sources of key indicative information at the margin of business.

It is also important for a leader to personally "dip" and keep in touch with what is happening at certain strategic intercept points of the business. This is another way of understanding what is happening at the margin. In our business, one of those points was where the service met the customer. During my term as CEO, one of the standards I set for myself was to talk with at least one customer and several of our service workers every week to listen and learn what was happening at the margin of our business. Our "We Serve Day"—one day each year when every employee, no matter his or her job or title, was expected to participate in delivering one of our services—was designed to keep all our people in touch with the needs of our customers and those who were delivering our services.

Knowing your business at the margin helps in defining the realities for determining growth expectations, especially as budgets are developed. One year, as I was reviewing our business with Warren Buffett, an important shareholder, I was trying to explain why one of our units was forecasting only ten percent growth for the coming year when our standard for the overall business was twenty percent. I told him that before budgets were finalized, I thought I could get the team leading this unit to look at the possibility of a twelve percent or fifteen percent growth rate. He looked at me and said: "Bill, why would you do that? The market they are in isn't growing. An eight percent growth would be a great result. Remember, it's not how hard you row the boat, it's how fast the stream is moving." He was helping me to define reality. I realized I had not been close enough to this unit to understand how slow the stream was moving.

Knowing the business at the margin is also helpful in determining when and where to initiate change. Change is inevitable. Tomorrow is always different than today. Doing what you did yesterday will not always take you to where you need to be tomorrow. Some of your business lines are always in the process of becoming yesterday's breadwinners. Change and innovation are necessary to keep growing.

The people out making it happen every day are often the experts at knowing what changes need to be made. Leaders have to provide an environment for innovation and change, with elbow room for mistakes and with the recognition that if a thing is worth doing, it is worth doing poorly to begin with. New ideas may look good on the planning board, but only when you get started can you test them with customers. Not every new idea will be a good idea, and some of them will have to be shut down. As Drucker reminds us, "A dead corpse doesn't smell any better the longer you keep it around."

There are times as a leader when you find yourself in the middle of a crisis. The unexpected happens or a slow-burning fire turns into an explosive event. Being able to define reality is of critical importance in determining what decisions need to be made and in communicating what happened and what action has to be taken.

Several months after I came back into the CEO role at Service-Master as the result of the illness of my partner, two relatively minor issues suddenly became major issues. One involved a business unit that had experienced slow growth and then suddenly reported a big operating loss. The other involved a lawsuit that had been pending for several years. After a short trial, a jury had rendered a verdict against us and awarded the plaintiff a relatively small amount of compensatory damages but a large amount (more than $100 million) of punitive damages.

The news of both events hit at about the same time. What had gone wrong? Why were we surprised with these results? We were a public company. News releases had to be issued. The news would affect the value of our stock. What would I say to our shareholders, to the investment community, to our people? What needed to be done to correct these situations? How would these events affect the future of our company? The answers to these questions and the decisions that needed to be made all required the defining of reality. Time was short.

The news of the loss in the business unit came just before the close of the quarter. While the operating loss was not large enough to change what we had previously projected for the quarterly earnings of the entire company, it did have a potential impact on whether we should take a write-down of the intangible assets of this business unit.

As I listened to the alternative views of our accountants and our outside auditors, including their review of the various methods of computing the present value of these intangible assets, it was clear that some methods of valuation would support a conclusion that no write-down would be necessary. I also realized that if we did take a write-down, we would report a down quarter in profitability for the first time in more than twenty years. I also knew this business unit would probably not be part of our future and that we should consider selling it within the next year.

As part of defining reality and determining what decision should be made, I asked the operating leader responsible for this business unit some simple but direct questions: "If we sold the business today, what could we sell it for? And how would we, or the buyer, value these intangible assets?" His answers led all to agree that a major write-down should be taken. Reality was defined and a decision, although difficult, was made. We also decided that steps would be taken within the next twelve months to sell this business unit.

The second issue involved a meeting with our in-house attorneys and the attorneys representing us at the trial. I was advised that the trial judge had a bias against large public companies and that he had determined in the middle of the trial to strike our answer and deny us the opportunity to present our defense to the claims of the plaintiff. So the case had gone to the jury with only the claims of the plaintiff.

Our in-house counsel also advised me that some of the actions and statements of our trial attorneys had alienated the judge. Both attorneys were confident the decision of the judge and the jury, including the large punitive damage award, would be reversed on appeal. Although I left that meeting with concern over the way we had been represented, I had taken time before the meeting to read some of the trial record, and it was clear to me that the judge had acted inappropriately. A decision was made to appeal.

In seeking to define reality, I could communicate to the public, our shareholders, and our people that we were confident the decision of the trial court would be reversed on appeal. In the next twelve months, we achieved that result and were able to settle the case with the payment of a reasonable amount.

Talking to God

During this time of crisis, I specifically sought God's guidance in my decision-making. For me, as a Christian, prayer is a vital link in developing my relationship with God. One of the privileges I have had has been working with Billy Graham and participating as a board member of the Billy Graham Evangelistic Association and as chairman of its executive committee. Billy has been a mentor to me by his words of encouragement and advice, and by the example of his life, including his prayer life. His continued focus on prayer and the study of God's Word has provided direction in his life and ministry. Fame and popularity have not distracted him from a single-minded calling, preaching and sharing of the Gospel of Jesus Christ—the good news of salvation for all who will receive it.

Billy's genuineness and his passion for the physical and spiritual welfare of others confirm the reality of his message. He has been not only a good preacher but a great leader. The organization he has led reflects his integrity. His leadership has not been about promoting self but about promoting the Gospel.

Along the way, he faced criticism from those of other faiths and ideologies. Some also came from other Christians. He dealt with detractors by sticking to his message rather than trying to answer his critics. C. S. Lewis said of Billy during a meeting they had in 1954, "You have many critics but I have never met one of your critics who knows you personally."

Some have suggested that Billy Graham has a spiritual aura about him. I would never describe it as such; however, I would say this about him: there has never been a time when I have visited with him—in his office, in his home, in a hotel room, in a hospital room—when there hasn't been an open Bible he had been reading just before I came. And before I left, he would either close our time with prayer or ask me to do so. Knowing God and being known by Him has been Billy's strength.

Billy Graham, God's messenger of the good news of the Gospel, taking the time to share from his open Bible with some of my grandchildren.

Deciding and Delegating

Leaders make decisions. Good decisions are often based not on all we know at the time, but on the steps of implementation we build into a decision at the time it is made.

Many of the decisions made by leaders are based not on facts but on other people's opinions or perceptions of the facts. This was the reason why Drucker suggested we need some disagreement about what should be done as part of testing the perceptions upon which we are basing our decisions. In making decisions, we should always seek to resolve the generic issues. Otherwise, we may be dealing only with symptoms and not causes.

Although some decisions cannot be delegated by leaders, many can. Learn to delegate. It is an important part of the development of the people with whom you are working. At times, you may want to retain the right to approve before a decision is implemented, but in a well-run organization, leaders always push decision-making out to where the action is and as close as possible to those who understand how it will affect the customer.

My predecessor at ServiceMaster, Ken Wessner, was an expert in delegating. He did so in a manner that, when you walked away, you knew you were now responsible for making the decision, and you never wanted to let him down. I remember the day, about six months after I had been appointed CEO, when he came in to see me and to talk about how the business was doing. After ten minutes of talking about general trends in the business, he asked me about one of our major business units. I told him I had some concern, including whether this unit was going to meet its goals for the next quarter.

He said, "You are worried about whether the leader of that unit is making the right and necessary operating decisions, aren't you?" When I told him I was, he replied: "But Bill, that's not your job. It's the job of the person leading that business unit. He's got to make it happen. You have delegated that responsibility to him. I know you will feel the pain and accountability if he doesn't meet his goals, but you are no longer operating that business unit. You are the CEO of the entire company. You've got to start thinking about where this company is going to be three years from now, five years from now, not just the next quarter."

Ken then reminded me of the importance of the principle of subsidiarity, that *it is wrong to steal a person's right or ability to make a decision.* He said: "He's got the right to make the operating decisions. See to it that he feels the responsibility to make them and to meet the goals he has set. If he doesn't, then you have to make the decision about whether he should be removed."

Ken went on to point out some of the strategic issues before us if we were to maintain our growth momentum: "Bill, we are going to need another growth curve. What that will be is your decision and it's your responsibility to make it happen." It was another one of those great moments of learning from a mentor who was a good teacher and a great leader.

Soul Craft

There is much more I could say about the awesome responsibility of leadership, but most of it has already been said in the other books I have written. Let me close with the story about Maria and a question for you.

Maria joined the ServiceMaster family as a housekeeper doing menial cleaning tasks in a long-term care facility we served in the Chicago area. At the time, she spoke only Spanish. She had no prior regular work experience and had limited formal education, but she did have a desire to learn. She had empathy for others. She wanted to do something significant. She had hope.

Maria accomplished much in her ServiceMaster career, not just for herself but also for her teammates and customers. She soon became a supervisor, then a manager, and then led the ServiceMaster program in several health care facilities and school districts in Illinois, Wisconsin, and Texas. She became proficient in English and mastered college-level courses in accounting, history, and English literature. In her career, she accomplished not just work objectives, but also important family objectives, including supporting her aging mother. People have cared for Maria along the way, and her response has been loyalty to the firm and leadership in providing excellent service to the customer.

While most of what I have just said about Maria was in my book *The Soul of the Firm*, the following comments she sent to me after that book was published confirm that she had become a leader with a sincere care for the people who followed her and a deep gratitude for those who had invested in her. She told me: "Leadership is much more an art, a belief, a condition of the heart than a set of things to do. I have had many mentors in ServiceMaster and their care has benefitted me and helped me develop my leadership skills and loyalty to the company and its objectives."

The world is filled with Marias. Our job as leaders and managers is simply to identify them and provide an environment in which they can be nurtured, grow, and develop. In so doing, we are participating in what I refer to as soul craft—the soul of the person and the soul of the firm.

So, will the leader please stand up? Not the person with the title of president, but the role model. Not the highest-paid person in the firm, but the risk taker. Not the person with the most perks, but the servant. Not the person who is the promoter of self, but the promoter of others. Not the maintainer, but the initiator. Not the taker, but the giver. Not the talker, but the listener. People want effective leadership, leadership they can trust, leadership that will nurture their souls, leadership that will make a difference in achieving meaningful results.

The workplace is not just where we get things done. It is also a place that can become a moral community for the development of the human character. A community that reflects a responsibility for its people and a care for those they serve. A community where it is okay to raise the question of God.

I have retired from my leadership responsibilities at ServiceMaster. As I look back, I can add up the numbers that show growth in profits, customers served, and a return for our shareholders averaging twenty percent a year. While these figures are part of a normal business assessment of performance, the conclusion for me cannot be limited to money or value-creation measurements. The real and lasting measurement is whether the results of my leadership can be seen in the changed and improved lives of the people I led as they had the opportunity to grow and develop in their work and respond to the reality of God and His redeeming love for each one of them. We are all prisoners of our hope. It is our hope that sustains us. It is our vision of what could be that inspires us and those we lead.

If you are currently in a leadership position, or you are ready to assume such a role, the choice will be yours. Will you lead or mislead? Will you invite God to be with you?

Ships are safe in the harbor, but that is not what ships are built for.

6

The Battlefield of the Market, Mind, and Soul

Ships are safe in the harbor, but that is not what ships are built for.

UNKNOWN AUTHOR

What is a market-driven economy supposed to accomplish? It certainly is not a safe harbor. It contains conflicting tides and currents, and has some of the characteristics of a battlefield. It is dependent, and should be, on competitive forces that result in winners and losers. The needs and wants of customers are always changing. Innovation and growth are essential for survival, but they also can contribute to failure and what the noted economist Joseph Schumpeter called "creative destruction."

Profit is the engine that drives a free market. It is the source for generating the required capital to innovate, grow, and satisfy the needs and wants of customers. For the business firm, it is often considered as a measure of effectiveness. However, it also can become an all-consuming force that nurtures a spirit of greed and has the potential to corrupt the mind and bankrupt the soul.

When markets function at their best, they fuel economic

growth and benefit a broad spectrum of people. While some may benefit and acquire more wealth than others, a rising tide raises all ships and the average standard of living increases. The problem is that not everyone owns a ship, and the average seems far away from a person at the bottom.

And what happens when markets fail to function effectively, resulting in no growth or a shrinking economy; when there are more losers than winners? As we have recently witnessed, in such cases people lose jobs, home foreclosures increase, bankruptcies go up, and credit markets close down. Is there someone to blame for these results or are they just the inevitable outcomes of up and down cycles of a market-driven economy?

Wasn't it Adam Smith, in his treatise *The Wealth of Nations*, who originally stirred our thinking about the positive potential of a market-driven economy? He suggested that an "invisible hand" would guide the system, causing the self-interest of the profit seeker, along with the discipline of competition, to benefit society as a whole by providing needed goods and services at the lowest possible price.

But where was this invisible hand in the last market downturn? Wasn't it the self-interest of profit-seeking Wall Street barons who packaged and sold subprime mortgages that contributed to the negative result? And what about the self-interest and greed of those executives who took bonuses and excessive compensation, then bailed out as their economic ships were sinking?

One response is to say there ought to be laws against such actions. But do we need more of the "visible" hand of government to provide added regulations? The intervention of government can be helpful in certain situations to provide more stability and incentives for growth. But while additional laws and rules of compliance may bring a higher standard of accountability and curb certain behaviors, legislative actions cannot assure honesty, integrity, or the assumption of a moral responsibility for the welfare and interest of others. In fact, as we witnessed in the twentieth century, when governments assume too much control over markets, economies fail and poverty increases.

But the market concerns today are not just about too much government control; they are also about government's ineptness in resolving its own economic problems of balancing budgets and reducing debt. As a result, there is a pall of uncertainty that has a chilling effect on investment and economic growth.

Despite all its imperfections, we should acknowledge that a market-driven economy, sometimes referred to as "capitalism" or "the free market," is the most effective way to produce needed goods and services while creating wealth and raising the standard of living for the people affected. We should also recognize, however, that it is morally neutral. It is indifferent to moral choices. It is materialistic and impersonal. It can result in great human blessings as well as great human misery.

A Moral Reference Point

The market needs a moral reference point beyond the system itself. Such a moral reference point must come from the people who make markets work. As we have discussed in previous chapters, people have, as part of their humanity, a moral and a spiritual dimension, with a conscience that accounts for a sense of what "ought" and "ought not" to be done.

But people always have a choice. They can nurture and respond to their moral and spiritual dimension or suppress and resist it. They can be right or wrong, good or evil, honest or dishonest, prudent or selfish. People can recognize God as their Creator and their source for a moral standard or can reject Him and His way.

As we conduct business in a pluralistic society, can we agree on a source of moral authority? Is there a moral standard for the ethos of the business firm, a standard that would provide guidance and constraint for what might otherwise become a fragmented center of self-interest? Can the business firm produce needed goods and services for a profit, create wealth for its shareholders, and also become a moral community for the development of human character? A community where people find purpose and meaning in their work? A community that encourages a strong ethic to be other orientated, a care of family, a willingness to give back, a practice of charity, an engagement in diversity, a capacity to resist the lure of hedonism and greed, a sense of discipline, a commitment to truth and justice, a desire to learn and acquire more knowledge, a respect for the dignity and worth of others regardless of rank, title, position, or wealth, and a willingness to serve as part of leading?

In his classic work *The Protestant Ethic and the Spirit of Capitalism*, Max Weber concluded that the Protestant Reformation was one of the driving forces for the growth of capitalism. He also observed, however, that by the beginning of the twentieth century, the business organizations driving the market had assumed control over the worker. The worker had become a part of the machine of production, trapped in what Weber described as the "iron cage" without hope of relating the specifics of the work task to the process of human development or the glorifying of God.

Now, more than a century later, is that "iron cage" still in the workplace? We talk about restructuring and reengineering work. We often use words such as *downsizing* and *rightsizing* to mask the reality that with the changing requirements of the job and the need for more knowledge workers, some people lose jobs for reasons other than performance.

Technology is allowing us to move work to where the worker is instead of always requiring the worker to come to a place of work. The computer and the smartphone provide communication and access to information from almost any location. This adds a virtual dimension to the work environment. People can do business with each other without ever experiencing personal contact or engagement.

The future will bring even more innovations in technology. Just one example: the differences in languages we experience today will not be the same barrier in the future. A computer program will do the translating.

The growing globalization of the market means that the business firm must learn to work within and among different cultures. Globalization will also create greater interdependence and less predictability among national economies. These changing dynamics will present new challenges in building community, especially a moral community.

Despite these challenges and changes, there continues to be a general agreement among economists that the economic and wealth-creation potential of the future will be more dependent on human capital than any other resource or source of capital.

In light of the importance of this human factor, we need, as I mentioned in chapter 3, a transformation in how business firms are led and how future business leaders are taught. Crafting a culture of character requires leaders to understand the essence of their own human nature and the human nature of those they lead. They must possess a strong moral fiber and know their source of moral authority.

Robert Fogel, a Nobel Prize-winning economics professor from the University of Chicago, supports the need for this moral leadership. In his book *The Fourth Great Awakening*, he traces the history of religious faith in America from pre-Revolutionary War times to the present. He analyzes the effect of religion and moral values upon issues in our society, businesses, and the economy. He concludes that one of the biggest challenges in today's culture is not the lack of employment opportunities, the distribution of economic resources, or the lack of diversity or equal opportunity. In his opinion, it is the lack of what he refers to as the distribution of spiritual assets. He concludes there is a void in our society in the development of the character of people.

How, then, do we determine the moral standards to be promoted and adhered to for the development of character in the changing world of the twenty-first century? Our places of worship, our educational institutions, and our families should continue to be primary sources for this development. However, a number of these institutions are under stress, and some have limited their direct involvement in character or moral development, accepting a standard of tolerance that has little or no interest in determining what is right and wrong.

Since businesspeople spend most of their waking hours in the workplace, why shouldn't the development of human character and the teaching of moral behavior also be an integral part of this environment? Since there are growing expectations and legal requirements for the workplace to be inclusive and to become a place where we attempt to correct some of society's imbalances by providing economic opportunities and a level playing field for race and gender, why shouldn't we also be about character development?

Is there room for God as a source of moral authority in this battlefield of the market, mind, and soul—a battlefield that involves our pocketbook and our thought life, a battlefield that often has an unseen enemy who tempts us to measure victory by temporal rather than eternal standards? Is there anything in common between God and profit? Do we dare mix the two worlds of the sacred and the secular?

Is It One World or Two?

Some thought leaders have suggested that there is a basic conflict between spiritual values and economic objectives. They question whether capitalism and a faith such as Christianity can co-exist and have inferred that a significant number of religious leaders now believe they cannot. For them, the gap between the haves and the have-nots is one of the principal points of conflict. They conclude that profit and wealth are generated by some only at the expense of others; thus, there is no morality in such a system. Absent an equitable distribution or "handout" of the wealth to those in need, there can be no fairness or justice in a market-driven economy.

Others have gone so far as to say that ethics has no relevance to the way markets and businesses are conducted today. They conclude that, in the market, money and wealth are the only measures of a person's value. They say there is no room for the consideration of the moral standards of wisdom, temperateness, and other virtues. They further suggest that if businesspeople are serious about ethics or morality, they should recognize that deference to wealth is a vice; otherwise, there will continue to be two different worlds with two different views of doing good.

To me, these conclusions start with that faulty assumption that wealth and surplus value can be generated only at someone's expense. In making those assumptions, there is a failure to recognize that it is not a zero-sum world and wealth can be created as a result of discovery, innovation, and productivity, with a resulting benefit to society as this "new" wealth contributes to a growing economy.

As Benjamin Friedman points out in his book *The Moral Consequences of Economic Growth*, the growth of an economy means a rising standard of living for the clear majority of citizens and more often than not fosters greater opportunities, diversity, social mobility, a commitment to fairness, and a dedication to democracy.

He further notes that ever since the enlightenment, Western thinking has regarded these tendencies positively and has described them explicitly in moral terms.

Friedman also points out that, even with the collapse of Communism, among some, including religious leaders, there continues to be a romantic socialism that focuses on the undesirable aspects of the marketplace and economic expansion. Thus, they justify their position in moral terms. Friedman concludes that when a society becomes more open, tolerant, democratic, and prudent on behalf of generations to come, it is simply not true that moral considerations argue against economic growth.

Regarding the role of religion in understanding wealth and economic growth in moral terms, Friedman reviews the importance of the Reformation, including John Calvin's notion that wealth can be a blessing from God. He also points out the views of Calvin and Martin Luther that, in addition to being economically productive, work can also be a calling of God to fulfill one's duty in worldly affairs. As such, work is an explicitly moral undertaking.

Moral or Amoral? God or No God?

George Soros has made a lot of money and has given much of it away to charitable causes that reflect his personal philosophy. Also, at times, he has generated wealth at the expense of many. For example, as the result of his trading activities in currencies, he has been blamed for past collapses of the currencies of Thailand, Malaysia, Indonesia, Japan, and Russia.

During a 1998 interview on *60 Minutes*, the interviewer asked Soros about his views on the market and about God. The interviewer suggested there appeared to be an inherent contradiction at the center of George Soros. On the one hand, he was a capitalist who did not care about the social consequences of his actions. On the other hand, he was a philanthropist who cared about social consequences.

Soros responded by saying that in the market he had to compete and win, but as a human being, he was concerned about the society in which he lived. He said, "It's one person, who at one time engages in amoral activities and then the rest of the time tries to be moral."

To help viewers understand Soros, the interviewer then explained that Soros had been born in Budapest, Hungary, to parents who were wealthy, well-educated, and Jewish. When the Nazis occupied Budapest in 1944, George's father was a successful lawyer. Knowing there would be problems ahead for the Jews, he decided to split up his family. He bought forged papers and bribed a government official to take fourteen-year-old George into his family and swear he was his Christian godson. Survival, however, carried a heavy price. While hundreds of thousands of Hungarian Jews were being shipped off to death camps, George accompanied his phony godfather on his appointed rounds, confiscating property from Jews. Soros suggested in the interview that it was then, when he was fourteen, that his character was made.

The interviewer, who was unsure what Soros meant by that statement, reminded George that he had gone out with his protector and, in fact, helped him in the confiscation of property from the Jews. The interviewer concluded by saying this experience would have sent lots of people to the psychiatric couch for many years, and asked Soros if it was difficult for him. Soros said no; it created no problem for him, no feeling of guilt. In fact, he compared it to his work in the markets.

"If I weren't there doing what I was doing," he said, "somebody else would be taking it away, so I had no sense of guilt." In response to a follow-up question, he confirmed he was not religious and did not believe in God.

Soros apparently lives in two worlds, neither of which includes God. Can his seeking to do good in one justify his actions in the other or have a redemptive value? Should we accept his view of an amoral world in the marketplace, with no concern about being moral as we do business?

Some people of faith also find themselves living a bifurcated life—church on Sunday, work on Monday. The truth and moral principles of their faith are left in the pew on Sunday. Christians should be ambassadors of Christ, and as they do so, they should seek to integrate the claims of their faith with the demands of their work and be examples of moral behavior.

In June 2012, Dan Cathy, a Christian and a friend who is the CEO of Chick-fil-A, found himself the subject of headlines across America. In an interview, Dan shared his views relating to a commitment to operate Chick-fil-A in a way consistent with biblical values, which included support of the traditional family as defined in the Bible. Those seeking to legalize same-sex marriage made his comments a *cause célèbre*. Several politicians jumped on the bandwagon and said they would oppose approvals for any expansion of Chick-fil-A in their cities.

Then the American Civil Liberties Union issued a statement confirming that Dan and the company had the freedom and right to express their views and that political officials could not use their power to restrict this freedom or to limit the company's expansion because of the views of its CEO on marriage. Former Arkansas Governor Mike Huckabee suggested that people who were in agreement with Dan should celebrate that agreement by being good customers of Chick-fil-A on August 1, 2012. That day saw an outpouring of customer support that may have resulted in the biggest revenue day in the company's history.

In the process of doing business, Dan raised the issue of what constitutes a marriage, and in his answer he stated his source of moral authority. If a business wants to be involved in the moral development of people, it cannot ignore an issue like this.

God in the Public Square

This incident involving Dan Cathy and Chick-fil-A confirms the reality that tolerance is a two-sided coin. As we seek a society of openness and inclusiveness, we should not abandon or restrict the expression of people's convictions that there are standards of right and wrong or that God should be the reference point for determining those standards.

In the public square, there will always be debates about what those standards should be and whether there is an ultimate source for determining them. We should always allow that debate to occur, and Christians should be faithful in raising the question of God and the truth of His way as they seek to affirm their faith in a way consistent with what they believe. There may be times when the moral standards accepted by society and allowed by law are not consistent with the standards of the Christian faith. In such circumstances, Christians who serve in leadership roles must decide whether they can continue to serve in a way that affirms their faith but does not impose it.

People often avoid the question of God because they do not

want to offend. As I reflect upon this reality, I am reminded of an experience I had at the Harvard Business School. Because of the growth and development of our company, the uniqueness of our corporate objectives, including "To Honor God in All We Do," and our management style, the Harvard Business School developed several case studies on ServiceMaster. When the cases were being taught, the professor often invited me to participate, and during those times I often received questions from the students about our corporate objectives and how we implemented them.

One time a student asked me if we couldn't do everything we wanted to do at ServiceMaster without that first objective, "To Honor God in All We Do." She said we must be offending people with that objective and wondered if we really needed it.

At Harvard, you can't just say no to a question like this. You also have to give a reason for your no. In my response, I said that the objective had a valid purpose, if only for her to have asked the question. God, and whether or not He exists, and what role, if any, He plays in determining how one lives and treats others are major questions of life that every person must face. I told her that, as a Christian, I had accepted God's offer of redemptive love and that I believed God had created every person with dignity and worth, as well as the freedom to choose, including the freedom to believe or not believe in God and His ways. My faith in God provided me a source of authority; an ultimate standard for what is right and wrong, and a guide for the way I should treat people and conduct business. I ended my answer with a rhetorical question: "What is your choice of a moral authority for determining these ultimate questions of life?" The question of God is a basic question of life. We cannot avoid it. All of us will respond to it in one way or another before we die.

In a recent book entitled *We Don't Do God*, George Carey, the former archbishop of Canterbury, discusses this issue and expresses concern with some of the recent secular and legal trends in England that seek to exclude expressions of faith from the public square. Some believe that matters of faith and religion should be kept private—practiced in the home, church, synagogue, or mosque, but not in the public square. Therefore, a person should not wear a cross around his neck when he comes to work. In fact, he can be fired if he persists in doing so. Neither should a person offer to pray for a fellow worker or express the conclusion that same-sex marriage is not consistent with the teaching of the Bible.

While the "jury" is still out on whether some of the lower court rulings denying the right to express religious views in public will be upheld in England, there is a growing attitude in most Western societies that matters of faith should be kept private. But the question of God is not a private matter. It is even relevant to subjects such as economic growth and the free-market system. As Greg Forster, a PhD from Yale and author of several books, reminds us in his essay, "Greed Is Not Good for Capitalism," it is God's standard that we are to be responsible stewards of all He has provided. Forster believes this principle is essential to understanding the history of economic growth and its potential for the future. He concludes that economic growth is both a moral and spiritual enterprise.

What Does Jesus Say?

So is there room for God in this battlefield of the market, mind, and soul? Is there room for business firms to be moral communities for the development of human character and to raise the question of God in so doing? We have reviewed what others have to say on this subject. Now let's take a look at what Jesus said about money and wealth, God and profit:

Words of Jesus

"Do not lay up for yourselves treasures on earth, where moth and rust destroy and where thieves break in and steal, but lay up for yourselves treasures in Heaven. . . . For where your treasure is, there your heart will be also" (Matthew 6:19–21).

Context

Jesus is discussing His views of life with His disciples in what is known as the Sermon on the Mount.

Principle

Our earthly possessions and wealth have no eternal value unless they are invested and used for God's purposes.

Moral Hazard

Do we need what we have or do we have what we want? Failure to use and invest the surplus of what we have for God's purposes is a waste and a sin.

Business Application

We should invest in the growth and development of people producing a beneficial and profitable service or product by focusing on who they are becoming, as well as what they are doing. This contributes to their dignity and worth, honors their Creator, and has the potential for an eternal return.

Words of Jesus

"Take care, and be on your guard against all covetousness, for one's life does not consist in the abundance of his possessions" (Luke 12:15).

Context

After Jesus spent time with the Pharisees and a large crowd of people, He made this comment to His disciples.

Principle

As created beings, we are immortal. There is a life beyond this world. Our actions and choices here will determine the people we are becoming and who we will ultimately be.

Moral Hazard

The ruler we use to measure what others possess is always too short, and a desire to have what they have can poison the soul.

Business Application

We should focus on creating and keeping customers by satisfying their needs with value and excellence. We should not limit our focus to what competitors have or do not have. As we serve and provide customers with value and excellence, we honor God.

Words of Jesus

"For what will it profit a man if he gains the whole world and forfeits his soul?" (Matthew 16:26).

Context

This statement is part of a talk Jesus had with His disciples about His coming death and resurrection.

Principle

Profit as an end goal of life is an empty vessel, whereas a choice for a relationship with God has eternal value.

Moral Hazard

Enough is never enough. An insatiable appetite for the tangible things of this world will result in poverty of the soul.

Business Application

We should not be consumed with maximizing profit. Instead, we should develop a purpose for our business that extends beyond the bottom line.

Words of Jesus

"So whatever you wish that others would do to you, do also to them" (Matthew 7:12).

Context

This statement also comes from the Sermon on the Mount.

Principle
Life is never lived alone. Each of us has the responsibility to develop relationships with others and to act toward them the way we would like to be treated. Every person is created in the image and likeness of God and has his or her own fingerprints of potential.

Moral Hazard
We are prone to limit our investment in others to what we expect from them in return.

Business Application
Business growth is never the result of one person. It always takes a team effort to succeed. We should always be willing to buy what we sell, to never ask someone to do something we are not willing to do ourselves, and to serve as part of leading.

Words of Jesus

"I say to you, only with difficulty will a rich person enter the kingdom of Heaven" (Matthew 19:23).

Context
Jesus made this comment after talking with a rich young man who was not willing to give up his wealth to follow Jesus.

Principle
Wealth is an insufficient measure of who we are and what we are capable of accomplishing.

Moral Hazard
When wealth becomes a dominant measurement for the value of life, we lose sight of the eternal wealth of a relationship with God.

Business Application
We should integrate our faith with our work and keep our eyes on *the* priority of life.

The Tides of Life

Words of Jesus

"For it will be like a man going on a journey, who called his servants and entrusted to them his property. To one he gave five talents, to another two, to another one, to each according to his ability. . . . Now after a long time the master of those servants came and settled accounts with them. And he who had received the five talents came forward, bringing five talents more, saying, 'Master, you delivered to me five talents; here I have made five talents more.' His master said to him, 'Well done, good and faithful servant. You have been faithful over a little; I will set you over much.' . . . He also who had the two talents came forward, saying, 'Master, you delivered to me two talents; here I have made two talents more.' His master said to him, 'Well done, good and faithful servant. You have been faithful over a little; I will set you over much.' . . . He also who had received the one talent came forward, saying, 'Master, I knew you to be a hard man . . . I was afraid, and I went and hid your talent in the ground. Here you have what is yours.' But his master answered him, 'You wicked and slothful servant! . . . You ought to have invested my money with the bankers, and at my coming I should have received what was my own with interest. So take the talent from him and give it to him who has the ten talents'" (Matthew 25:14–28).

Context

Jesus shared this parable with His disciples near the end of His ministry, during discussions about the kingdom of God.

Principle

We are stewards, not owners, of the resources God has provided—our time, talent, and treasure—and we are to invest these resources for profitable returns with eternity in view. As the owner, God does not want us to give back what He has already given to us. He wants more. Profit is a virtue.

Moral Hazard

We can develop a mind-set of preservation with a failure to risk investing for a profitable and eternal return.

Business Application

The marketplace is made up of a diversity of people who represent the world that God so loves. We should invest our time, talent, and resources as faithful stewards in a way that honors God.

Words of Jesus

"And I tell you, make friends for yourselves by means of unrighteous wealth, so that when it fails they may receive you into the eternal dwellings" (Luke 16:9).

Context

These words of Jesus follow the parable of the unjust steward. This was a parable about a steward who, when he was found to have been unfaithful with his master's possessions, went out and reduced the amounts owed by his master's debtors so that when he lost his job, he would find favor with them. When the master found out what he had done, he commended the steward for being shrewd.

There are a number of interpretations as to what the unjust steward did. In my view, it appears that he initially overcharged the debtors or customers for what they received, intending to pocket the difference for himself. When he found out he was going to lose his job, he then forgave that difference and reduced the amount owed the master to what should have been originally charged.

Principle

As an end in itself, money and its accumulation are unrighteous. It has no eternal value. It is, however, an important means in this world to be used and invested for fulfilling God's purposes. To avoid or subordinate the earning and proper use of money is imprudent and inconsistent with faithful stewardship.

Moral Hazard

We can allow the making of money to consume us to the point that we lose sight of God and His ways.

Business Application

Christians in the marketplace are stewards of God's resources and should embrace and engage in the making of money for use in furthering God's purposes.

Words of Jesus

"One who is faithful in a very little is also faithful in much, and one who is dishonest in a very little is also dishonest in much. If then you have not been faithful in the unrighteous wealth, who will entrust to you the true riches? And if you have not been faithful in that which is another's, who will give you that which is your own?" (Luke 16:10–12).

Context

This is additional follow-up teaching of Jesus on the parable of the unjust steward.

Principle

It is required of a steward that he or she be found faithful.

Moral Hazard

We can lose the trust of God and the opportunity to invest for God and others by being unfaithful.

Business Application

As we are being productive, we should also be faithful, just, caring, and free of arrogance or self-aggrandizement.

Words of Jesus

"No servant can serve two masters, for either he will hate the one and love the other, or he will be devoted to the one and despise the other. You cannot serve God and money" (Luke 16:13).

Context

Jesus closes the discussion of the parable of the unjust steward with this truth.

Principle

There is an unavoidable conflict of interest in seeking to serve both God and money. There can be only one end goal of life for the Christian, and that is to seek and serve the will and way of God. Money is one of the means we can use to accomplish this end goal.

Moral Hazard

In our attempt to excel in whatever we do, including business, we can allow what is temporal to become controlling and override what is eternal.

Business Application

We can honor God in business by focusing on the end goals of life and by using the means goals, including money and profit, to serve His purposes. These words of Jesus don't apply just to Christians. They have a general application to everyone doing business. Everyone should:

- Be faithful stewards
- Recognize and honor the dignity and worth of people
- Be other-oriented and not controlled by selfish desires
- Focus on *the* priority of life
- Understand the difference between end goals and means goals
- Seek a meaningful purpose for work and be profitable and productive in performing it
- Know their source of authority for determining right and wrong
- Determine their response to the question of God and whether they will choose to have a relationship with Him.

A Moral Community for the
Development of Human Character

Our business model at ServiceMaster not only included seeking to excel at serving customers, but it was also about the growth and development of people. We were an open and inclusive community that raised the importance of the question of God and the choices we had in responding to that question.

The following excerpt from a letter to the editor of *The Wall Street Journal* reflects how one of our frontline managers responded to our company culture:

> Our society has become too secular, too amoral. . . . Our economic life is probably the most secular facet of our society. Fortunately, I work for a company that is non-secular and proud of it—ServiceMaster. Reference to God in our company objectives gives us an ethical framework for business behavior.

As I read this in the *Journal*, I realized once again the importance of raising the question of God in our business and considering His role in determining standards for moral behavior.

We did not use the first objective—"To Honor God in All We Do"—as a basis of exclusion. Instead, it became the reason for our promotion of diversity, as we recognized that different people with different beliefs were all part of God's mix. The business firm must operate in a diverse and pluralistic world. It is not the role of the firm to mandate a person's beliefs. It is not a church or a place of worship.

The business firm as a moral community must be inclusive and should encourage the freedom to explore truth, including raising the question of God and His redemptive role in transforming the lives of people. The ultimate litmus test that should be acceptable to all as a way to judge a business firm's moral standards or actions is their effect upon people.

Much about our business could be considered by some as routine or mundane. We often dealt with people in entry-level positions. Some were unskilled, uneducated, and more often than not unnoticed. Our task was to train, motivate, and develop these people so they could do a more effective job, be more productive in their work, and also be better people. This was both a management and a leadership challenge, which was far from being mundane.

This ethic of seeking to be a moral community required the recognition that people were not economic animals or non-personal production units. Every person had his or her own fingerprint of personality and potential. We believed the work environment could be a place where the spirit and soul of people could be enriched by what they did as they learned more about their own potential and as they served and contributed to others.

The question for us was whether people were growing as individuals who could contribute not only in their work environment, but also in other areas of life. Stressing this value affected our view of the importance and scope of the training and learning process in the work environment. Training was more than teaching people to use the right tools and to complete an assigned task within a defined period. It also involved how they felt about their work and about themselves, and their contribution to the well-being of the person being served, whether the customer was a patient, a student, or a homeowner. This meant that those in management, as part of their training, should experience what it was like to do the hands-on work and to feel the emotions of those they were managing.

We viewed the process of learning as a lifelong experience. The scope of our teaching and learning process ranged from how to mop a floor to the skills of management and leadership, which included a ServiceMaster MBA program. We believed in the teacher/learner process and determined that if you were too busy to teach, you were too busy to work for us.

This ethic also placed value on a job well done. Work provided people the opportunity to develop and serve others. In the absence of a job well done, others had to make up the difference or there was a loss or expense to those being served. Work became a vehicle for understanding the important lesson that our actions affected others.

Our ethic and way of doing business also recognized the value of the family as the basic spiritual, economic, and social unit for the welfare of society. We conducted business in such a way as to encourage the family unit. Spouses were typically involved in the initial interviewing process and were also invited to be involved in business meetings and other company affairs. We encouraged social relationships among our employees and the inclusion of children in understanding the parent's work environment. This was not just good business; it was the right thing to do.

There was another value that flowed from our desire to be a moral community. It was the value of covenants and commitments as a basis for the combined efforts of people in seeking to accomplish meaningful results. It was the value of a kept promise. An enterprise cannot function to its capacity unless its people can rely upon each other to keep the covenants and commitments they give to each other. Some are formalized in written agreements, such as employment contracts or contracts covering services to a customer. Others, usually more important, are oral promises or statements generating reliance or requiring action by another. The influence and binding characteristic of these oral covenants often go far beyond any legal document. They extend to those doing the day-to-day work of the firm, who are relying upon leaders to make the right decisions for their future. It is to these people that a leader is truly bound, without any formal contract, to provide continuing opportunities for them to develop and grow.

Leaders who accept this ethic must be prepared to be examples of another important value—the willingness to serve. Leaders must be willing to do what they ask others to do; to listen and learn before they talk; to walk the talk as role models and teachers; and to not be caught up in the perks of office, but to be givers, not takers.

At ServiceMaster, we also placed a value on the importance of profit as a means goal. It was a measurement of the effectiveness of our efforts. It provided a return for our shareholders, which included our employees, who had the opportunity to participate in the ownership of the firm as individuals and in their savings and retirement plans. Without surplus, there could be no economic growth or survival of the firm. For us, it was not a matter of maximizing profits; instead, we focused on a continuity of growth—a continuity that continued for more than fifty years and provided a growing value for our owners. As I have already said, profit viewed as an end in itself can foster greed and other abuses. It may result in some short-term economic benefits but rarely has a long-term benefit.

The firm that values the dignity and worth of the individual also must be committed to provide an environment for people to participate in the decision-making process and to "own" the results of their work and the overall results of the firm. The firm is dependent upon results and is obligated to those producing the results to provide a fair and equitable distribution of those results. The work environment should also allow elbow room for mistakes, for in the absence of grace, there will be no reaching for potential.

I will end this section with another important ethic of the firm—the value of truth and transparency in our dealings with others. This requires open and honest dealings with full disclosure. For people to have trust in the leadership of the firm, there must be a recognition of the importance of truth, and the leader must live a life that is consistent with what is said.

Bending Without Breaking

As I review these ethical principles that became an integral part of the way we did business, I freely admit they could not always be applied like a mathematical formula. At times, there were judgments to be made in their application, especially when a situation involved competing interests or values. There were occasions when it was wise to bend without breaking, to use an old Scottish term. Or, to put it another way, to accept half a loaf of bread rather than no loaf at all.

When I found myself in such situations, I always remembered the wisdom of Solomon when he was confronted by two women, each of whom claimed to be the mother of a baby. He suggested that the baby be cut in half so that each woman could have half a baby. At that point, one woman immediately protested and offered to give up her claim to save the life of the child. The other woman continued to insist upon her claim. When he heard their responses, Solomon knew who was the real mother and gave her the child (1 Kings 3:16–28).

When there are competing interests and a judgment has to be made as to whether to compromise in the application of an ethical or moral standard, make sure you are dealing with half a loaf of bread and not half a baby. Half a loaf is still bread; half a baby is no baby at all.

I faced such a judgment call during one of my travels to Japan. During a visit to our various business units, I received many questions about the meaning and application of our objective "To Honor God in All We Do." At the close of my visit, during a wrap-up session with the president of our Japanese partner, he told me that my remarks on this subject had caused him some problems. It had been a long-standing custom of our partner to start every day with a ceremony involving a song of commitment to serve the customer and then to end the ceremony with a Buddhist chant. As a result of my remarks, the Japanese Christians in the business were refusing to attend the daily opening ceremony and the president was going to have to order them to do so.

I asked if I could attend the ceremony the next morning. He agreed and asked me to say a few words at the conclusion.

The next morning, I was impressed by the enthusiastic chorus of the people as they committed themselves to serve the customer. I stood respectful and still during the Buddhist chant.

Learning from our Japanese partner the lesson of bending but not breaking.

Then it was my turn to speak. I shared with them the testimony of my faith and that earlier that morning I had prayed to a God who cared and listened. I told them I had asked that my words and actions of this day would reflect His love for them. I also explained why I believed that serving customers with excellence could honor God, even though some of those so serving might not believe in Him. The applause that followed indicated my remarks were favorably received.

Afterward, I had another meeting with the president and suggested a compromise. The Christians could attend the opening ceremony and participate in the chorus about serving the customer. They would remain respectful and silent during the Buddhist chant and then would be given, as I had that morning, an opportunity, if they chose to do so, to share something about their faith. He agreed. Although there were still differences in culture and faith, there would be opportunities for all to express the reality of our respective faiths and the love of God. The compromise resulted in half a loaf of bread and not half a baby.

As we implemented these ethical and moral standards, they

became a living set of principles allowing us to confront the difficulties and failures that were all part of life and the operation of a business. We did so with the assurance that our starting point did not change and provided a reason and hope beyond the differences and difficulties that were always present.

As Peter Drucker observed, we were becoming, in his terms, a community for the development of human character. As such, he concluded we were performing an important social function, one that went beyond providing society with needed goods and services. We were human change agents investing in human achievement, human growth, and human fulfillment.

Over the years, Peter prodded and encouraged me to promote the idea of the business firm as a moral community, not only within the world of ServiceMaster but beyond. He suggested I write a book, and the result was *The Soul of the Firm*. He was concerned about the lack of invigorating moral values in the teaching of business and suggested we should consider sponsoring a lecture series on the subject at some of the leading graduate schools of business. The result was the Hansen-Wessner Memorial Lecture Series, sponsored by ServiceMaster and held at the Drucker Management Center of the Claremont Graduate University, the Kellogg Graduate School of Management at Northwestern University, the Harvard Business School and Harvard Divinity School, the University of Notre Dame Business School, the Oxford University Business School, the Yale University Business School, the University of Southern California Business School, and the University of Michigan Business School.

All the lecturers were chosen by ServiceMaster, and each one was an effective business leader who had integrated the claims of his faith with the demands of his work and profession. They all knew the source of their moral authority and were committed to the development of human character as a key purpose of the firm. These lectures have been compiled in the book *The Heart of a Business Ethic*, edited by me and including a foreword by Warren Bennis.

Now that I have retired from leadership at ServiceMaster, I can look back and add up the numbers that show growth in profits, customers served, and increased value for our shareholders. While these figures are part of a normal assessment of business performance, for me the conclusion cannot be limited to such measurements. The lasting criterion—the criterion with eternal value—is whether the results of my leadership in the operation of the firm can be seen in the changed lives of people.

Three-Peat. A hat for John and for me as a reminder of our time together at the Bulls game.

As I close this chapter, I want to share a story of one of those people who was a part of the ServiceMaster team. John joined us in 1983 at the end of his senior year in high school. He had some special needs, but he also had a great desire to succeed and contribute. ServiceMaster crafted a job for him and provided him an opportunity to make a meaningful contribution in his work.

John's hiring was described by his mother and friends as a long-term investment by ServiceMaster and as a way of expressing the teaching of Jesus that "as you did it to one of the least of these My brothers, you did it to Me" (Matthew 25:40). It turned out to be a good decision for both parties.

I got to know John and we developed a personal friendship. Every time he saw me at work he was ready to give me the most recent scores of the local professional teams in Chicago. One night we went to a Bulls game together. It was an exciting experience for both of us.

John gave ServiceMaster his best efforts and undeniable loyalty. He knew no other way to conduct himself. In return, he received a fair wage and, more important, a sense of belonging, of contributing, and of identity. He was treated as the subject of work, not just the object of work. His family was also an important part of his contribution at ServiceMaster. Each and every work day, winter and summer, through family trials including the loss of his father, someone from the family would take him to work and pick him up when work was done.

After my retirement as CEO, my successor decided to sell the business unit that employed John. The purchaser continued to employ John, but had a different management style. The commitment to invest in John with sensitivity to his needs started to erode. One day, John's employment was terminated. When he was called in and told this, he was confused. He asked if he could say goodbye to some of his fellow employees and was told he could not. His manager had cleaned out his locker, and someone from the human resources department escorted him out the back door of the building.

The people of this firm were dutifully following a cold and clinical termination process with John, reflecting a mind-set that followed procedures without acknowledging the dignity and worth of the person or the value of what he had contributed. For ServiceMaster, John not only had done his job, but had done it in a way that overcame some of his limitations and was an inspiration to others. Even though his termination and the way it was implemented did not reflect it, John had grown and developed as a person during his time with ServiceMaster and had benefited the people he worked with, including me.

Did the decision to terminate John and the way it was handled reflect the actions of a moral community? Was it a community that embraced care and empathy for the dignity, worth, and special needs of the terminated person? Where was the soul of this firm? Did my successor get the right price for the business he was selling but fail to understand the buyer's possible lack of a "soul" in the way people would be treated? Leadership is an awesome responsibility.

Christians are called to be in the world but not of the world. The marketplace provides a wonderful opportunity for us to engage those whom God so loves with the reality of the Christian faith, including the importance of practicing moral values and obligations. Neither the law, the government, nor the market economy will function properly without them. For Christians, their faith provides the assurance that God will have a firm hand on the tiller as their ship leaves the safety of the harbor. We each have a ship to sail. The choice of whether we will leave the harbor and whom we will depend upon for direction (ourselves or God) is up to each one of us. It is a freedom of choice that carries with it accountability for results.

Etched in stone on the floor of the chapel of Christ Church College at Oxford University are the words of John Locke, spoken over three hundred years ago: "I know there is truth opposite to falsehood[,] that it may be found if people will [search for it,] & is worth the seeking."

On the battlefield of life and of the market, I believe there is victory for the mind and the soul from the One Who said, "I am the way, and the truth, and the life" (John 14:6).

7

Planning for the Future

Many are the plans in a man's heart,
but it is the LORD's purpose that prevails.

PROVERBS 19:21, NIV

John F. Kennedy was quoted as saying: "Change is the law of life. Those who look only to the past or the present are certain to miss the future." How do we prepare and plan for the future in a world of accelerated change? The only thing certain about tomorrow is that it will be different from today, and the differences beyond tomorrow continue to be more difficult to predict. It seems that in many areas of life we may be moving to a new normal involving greater ambiguity and uncertainty.

For example, previously accepted norms of right and wrong now seem to be subordinated to tolerance as the ultimate moral standard. Other moral standards have become matters of personal opinion, with no room for the ultimate authority of God. What is true or false no longer seems to be important as long as the differences between the so-called shades of truth and falsehood can be tolerated. While there is a value to being tolerant of different views when the views are supported by reason, if tolerance rules above all other moral standards, it results in an intolerance of faith in the authority of an unseen God. The role of God is reduced to the private view of a few, and there is no room for such a view in the public square for determining how we should then live.

Another example of what may be a new normal involves the expanding global marketplace, which has resulted in a growing economic interdependence among nation-states, causing more uncertainty, less predictability, and the potential of a diminishing role and influence for any one nation-state or national economy.

With the growing opportunities for manufacturing to move across national boundaries, how can we determine what is best for the world for the creation of jobs in the future? Should it be in China, to help develop a middle class and raise the standard of living for millions who are still living on less than $2 a day? Or should it be in the United States, one of the richest countries in the world, to reduce the unemployment rate and re-establish a manufacturing base? What is just and fair from a global viewpoint? And what about the growing global currency tensions as some nation-states take actions to push down their exchange rates to gain trade advantages? Will we continue to let "free" market forces seek to resolve these types of issues or will there be a move to have the United Nations or some other global governmental power resolve them?

A Future That Has Already Happened

Peter Drucker would often remind me that planning is not about predicting the future. It is pointless, he would say, to try and predict the future. It is possible, however, to identify the currents and trends in society, knowledge, culture, industry, government, and economic structures that have already happened and will affect tomorrow. Doing so will help us anticipate a future that has already happened and plan accordingly.

Some currents and trends may lead to a new normal and others may not. In addition to the two trends already mentioned, my summary of others includes:

1. The increasing impact of technology, creating more opportunities for people to communicate, learn, work, and do business
2. The demographics of a growing elderly population, resulting in increasing demands for support services, health care, and housing
3. The expanding economic gap between the haves and have nots
4. The mushrooming cost of government, with a continuing inability to pay for these costs from current income
5. The rising tides of tribalism and terrorism
6. The growing opportunity and need for innovative solutions

The Priority

Given these macro trends and currents that may affect our lives on a personal basis and the way we conduct business, where do we start? What are the priorities? Is there *a* priority?

During most of our planning periods at ServiceMaster, we sought advice from Drucker. At times, he spoke directly to our board of directors. At other times, he met with me and our senior management team. In advance of those meetings, we would provide Peter with our assessment of current trends that could affect the future and we would identify new opportunities for expanding our existing services to new markets and adding new services.

Peter would typically start our meetings with a critique of our thinking, adding his own perspective on current trends affecting the future and providing his opinion on what he called our breadwinners of tomorrow and our heroes of yesterday. With respect to the latter, he would also encourage us to initiate "organized abandonment."

At the conclusion of our sessions, I would try to summarize his comments as a way of capturing his wisdom and insights. During one of those summaries, I concluded my remarks by saying I thought Peter was telling us to do a better job of organizing our priorities. At that point, he interrupted me with a slap of his hand on the table and said with a forceful tone: "Bill, it's not about priorities. It's about *the* priority." He then gave us a history lesson on the use of the word *priority*. It came into the English language in the fourteenth century, he said, and it wasn't until the twentieth century that it was pluralized. He then went on to say:

> Bill, planning is not just thinking about the future or making a list of those things that could be done to make the future happen; but more importantly, it should help you focus on what should be done *now* to help make the future happen. You are in a period of explosive growth for the company. You have developed a strong and capable management team. Your priority now is to consider how best to invest your time at the "margin" of your business, where the service meets the customer. Listen to the people responsible to deliver the services. Listen to the customer. Get a fresh and direct understanding of their needs and wants and what has to be *done* to continue to improve the growth and development of your people and the quality of your service to the customer. Make this your priority. As you listen and learn at the edges of your business, you will also be better prepared to initiate the planning for that next major segment of your growth.

Once again, in just a few words, Peter hit the nail on the head.

His statement came at a time in my life when I personally felt very stretched. There were many moving parts in the business. In our planning, we were thinking of adding more services and expanding our international business. I was getting advice from several other sources about the need, on a personal basis, for more balance in my life, more time for my family, more time for church, and more time for healthy exercise.

Later that evening in my hotel room, as I reflected on Peter's comments, I realized his advice not only related to our business but also to me as a person. What was *my* priority? As I opened my Bible and began reading the chapters in Matthew known as the Sermon on the Mount, I came to verse 33 in chapter 6—a verse I had read many times before, but which now had a new emphasis and a special meaning for me: "But seek first the kingdom of God and His righteousness, and all these things will be added to you."

As a follower of Jesus Christ, this had to be my ultimate priority in life. If God wasn't in what I was doing, I should stop it. I was not the owner of my time; I was a steward of my time. I had the responsibility to invest my time, not just spend it. As I did so, it was not just about the *quantity* of time invested but also the *quality* of time. God's ultimate measure of my effectiveness would always be with eternity in view.

The process of planning for the future of our business provided me a renewed focus on the purpose and meaning for my life and faith. I was responsible for investing my life in serving others. This included my wife, my children, my friends, the people in our church, the people in our business, and the people we served by our business.

It was all about these people whom God so loved and for whom He gave His Son so they would have an opportunity to choose a relationship with Him. As I mentioned earlier, C. S. Lewis reminded us: "There are no ordinary people. You have never talked to a mere mortal. Nations, cultures, arts, civilizations—these are mortal, and their life is to ours as the life of a gnat. But it is the immortals whom we joke with, work with, marry, snub, and exploit."

Planning is a process that can help us understand not only what needs to be done for the future of the organizations where we work, but also the purpose and meaning for our personal lives. We should look beyond the circumstances of the present, reflect upon our hopes and beliefs about the future, and ask ourselves, "Where are we headed in this life and for eternity?"

As a Christian, my faith provides a hope for the future of this life and beyond. The Bible describes the Christian faith as "the assurance of things hoped for, the conviction of things not seen" (Hebrews 11:1).

God wants us to have a relationship with Him for now and eternity. For this relationship to be a reality, we must accept and embrace His offer of redemption and forgiveness. The choice is ours to make. Is there room for God in your life? Are you willing to explore and reflect upon those "things hoped for" and discover the reality of those "things not seen"?

Planning as a Way of Doing Business

Wise planning played a significant role in the growth and development of ServiceMaster. As I assumed the leadership of the company in the early 1980s, I inherited and benefitted from the contributions made to the planning process by my three predecessors: Marion Wade, Ken Hansen, and Ken Wessner.

Planning for the future had become a vital part of the way we did business. It inspired innovation, emphasized the imperative of growth, prepared people for change, enlisted commitment to the achievement of common objectives, and recognized the importance of embracing a mission and purpose that did not change.

As we ended the decade of the 1970s, Ken Wessner, who was then CEO of the company, had a view that our next planning cycle should include a twenty-year period. This would bring us to the onset of the twenty-first century. He realized, as we all did, that a twenty-year period would involve more changes than we could anticipate. For a business plan to have meaningful objectives, it would be necessary to divide the planning process into five-year planning segments. The longer twenty-year time horizon would provide a context for continuity and would help us understand the encore issues of what we were initiating and what we were discontinuing in each of the five-year segments. This planning process became known as SMIXX—ServiceMaster in twenty years.

As we entered our first planning segment, our annualized revenues were $400 million and our operating income was $27 million. Our largest and fastest-growing business unit provided management services for support departments in hospitals and other health care institutions. Our other business unit provided cleaning, disaster restoration, and janitorial services to the residential and commercial markets through a network of loyal and committed franchisees. This was the business we had started with as a company, and for more than thirty years it had generated good and steady growth.

As we concluded the final segment of the twenty-year planning period and entered the twenty-first century, our customer-level revenues had grown to more than $7 billion and our operating income exceeded $400 million. In addition to the services we were providing at the beginning of the period, we had also entered the educational and industrial markets with our management services, and we had grown to more than four thousand franchisees providing cleaning, disaster restoration, and janitorial services to the residential and commercial markets.

We also had added new services to serve these markets, including pest control, lawn care, landscaping, maid services, plumbing, and home warranty services. We had established more than eight thousand service centers and were making more than forty-five million service visits annually to more than eight million customers. Plus, we had expanded our various service lines to international markets, and with our international partners we were providing services in forty-five countries. We were employing and managing more than two hundred thousand people to deliver all these services.

We had become a big company. We had experienced both the joy of success and the pain of failure during this period. We had been recognized by *Fortune* magazine as the #1 service company of the Fortune 500, and were also included as one of its most admired companies. ServiceMaster was identified as a "star of the future" by *The Wall Street Journal* and recognized by the *Financial Times* as one of the most respected companies in the world.

However, as we entered the twenty-first century, we faced two major unanswered questions. The effective resolution, or lack thereof, of these questions would ultimately determine the future of ServiceMaster.

Planning as a Way of Seeking to Be Ahead of Change and Responding to the Reality of Entropy

The arrogance of success is to think that what you did to accomplish it in the past will be sufficient for the future. Continuing changes outside the firm—including those in the economy, competitive forces in market segments, and the needs and wants of customers—mean there is always a measure of what you are doing today that will not be relevant for tomorrow.

The imperative of growth requires that an organization must continually ask:

- What are we doing now that is no longer relevant for the future and must be abandoned?
- What are we doing now that is essential for the future and must be continued and improved?
- What are we not doing that we must start doing or acquire for a future of growth opportunities to continue?

The people who can best answer these questions are not always at the top of the organization or located in the strategic planning department. The people in the field, who are responsible for selling the services to new customers or managing the delivery of the services to existing customers, often have a better understanding of the changes in the market, the changing needs and wants of customers, and what is required to sell and serve non-customers. A good planning process needs to provide an open door for input from the front line.

Innovation and the entrepreneurial spirit naturally tend to deteriorate with each new major increment of growth. Structures and systems designed for uniformity and consistency in performance can sometimes discourage creativity. Organizations can become crippled by the cancer of bureaucracy, with too many layers of management defending the status quo. Drucker suggests these layers of management are like relay switches—with each new layer, there is more noise and less power.

A broad participatory and continuous planning process can become a vehicle to pierce these layers and provide opportunities for creative input from those who are closest to the customer and who are often more aware of new market opportunities.

Our decision to enter the educational market with our management services business was the result of just such input from one of our area managers. The chief administrative officer of one of his health care customers also served on a local school board. He wanted us to make a proposal to provide similar services to the school district. Although at first our area manager did not get much encouragement from corporate to proceed, he, along with his division leader, persisted and developed a plan to serve this school district. But they also had a vision and made a commitment to sell four more school districts before year-end.

Their initiative became the spark that started us in the education market. Five years later, this area manager had become the leader of a separate business unit of the company, serving more than 350 colleges, universities, and school districts in locations across the country and generating more than $400 million in annualized revenue. This was a great example of creative innovation by a frontline manager resulting in a new dimension of performance.

While encouraging innovation and creativity within the firm is important in identifying the new that should be added, it is also essential that the firm develop an organized way of reaching beyond its borders to identify changes occurring outside the organization that may affect its future.

As part of our research and development effort to look outside of ServiceMaster, we organized a separate venture fund to invest in small, entrepreneurial service companies that were seeking to combine the rapid changes in technology with the delivery of a more efficient and effective service. This venture fund not only produced an excellent financial return, but it also resulted in a partnership with Kleiner Perkins for the development of an online system for communicating with customers in our rapidly growing consumer services businesses. It changed the way we managed and delivered our services so that we could be more efficient, effective, and responsive.

Planning and anticipating what is needed for the future also requires identifying those things you are doing now that are no longer relevant for the future. Drucker referred to these as "yesterday's breadwinners." Organized abandonment is always painful for a business focused on success, but it is essential.

We found the following principles helpful in using planning as a way of staying ahead of change:

- Keep the organization open and flexible. This is a never-ending task.
- Learn to measure at the margin of your business, especially for your existing operations. For example, increases in your employee turnover rate may indicate people development or leadership issues. Decreases in your customer retention rate may reflect a growing quality issue or new competitive pressures. Understanding the marginal revenue/marginal cost curve for your business units or services provides an indicator of future profit trends.
- Test and pilot a new idea before you roll it out. If a thing is worth doing, it is worth doing poorly to begin with, so you can get started. You learn from mistakes during the piloting period, but you can't afford them once you roll the idea out and it gains scale.
- Give innovators elbow room for mistakes, but they also must be accountable and at risk for results. No firm can afford to have innovative consultants or bystanders.
- Develop an organizational structure that separates innovative initiatives from the main business units of the firm and protects the new idea from the crushing wheel of the firm's basic operations.
- As senior leadership, be supportive and ready to serve and listen, but also have the discipline to bury a failure. It is hard

for a successful firm to accept failure, but in Drucker's words, noted earlier, "A dead corpse doesn't smell any better the longer you keep it around."

Planning as a Continuous Reminder of "What Is Your Business?" and "What Is Your Core Competency?"

At the beginning of one of our planning sessions and before we had decided to expand into the consumer services market, Drucker spoke to our board of directors and senior management team about his views of the challenges and opportunities that were ahead of us.

Peter started the meeting with one of his famous questions: "What is your business?" The responses he received were about what we did in providing various services in different markets. After about five minutes of listening to these responses, mostly from our board members, he told them something I never could have said to them. He said:

> You are all wrong. Your business is the training and development of people. You are good at it. You package it in different ways to meet the needs of your customers, but you can't deliver a service without people and you can't deliver quality service without trained and motivated people.

He then reminded us of what Harvard professor Jim Heskett had said about ServiceMaster—that we had broken the cycle of failure for the service worker by focusing on the development of the whole person in the work environment and by providing meaning and purpose for even the most mundane tasks.

Peter commended us for our focus on developing the dignity of the service worker through ongoing training, motivation, and pride when a job was well done with improved productivity. He noted that this type of focus was sadly lacking during the industrialization of our country, when there was a growing number of blue-collar workers. He encouraged us to keep listening to our service workers on how tasks could be simplified and improved, and to continue involving them in assuming responsibility for the quality of their work and improvement in their productivity.

He concluded by emphasizing that the development of people in their work environment was our core competency, and that our future growth and expansion should build upon this competency. He knew we were considering expanding our services to a broader consumer market, and he noted that this should be a growing market for us because of the continuing trend toward two-wage-earner homes. He pointed out that the multiple services we could provide the homeowner not only would result in an improved quality of service, but would also have the value of freeing up time for the busy homeowner.

Peter's advice was confirming, as we would focus on the consumer services market as our next leg of growth. Significant changes lay ahead of us, including:

- Converting our legal structure from a corporation to a partnership to provide more cash for investment
- Purchasing Terminix and growing it into a market leader
- Acquiring Merry Maids, which already was a market leader with a well-developed franchise system
- Taking the risk of acquiring TruGreen and ChemLawn—two separate companies that were both losing money at the time we acquired them. But when combined and infused with good management and our people-development principles, they not only became the #1 provider of lawn care, they also became a major profit producer for the firm.
- Acquiring American Home Shield, which provided the homeowner with a warranty covering the cost of repair or replacement of appliances and heating and air conditioning equipment. The business model of American Home Shield was unique and added a special dimension to our service capability and customer base.

As we concluded the final segment of our SMIXX planning period, our consumer services business had grown to represent our largest business segment. It provided another extension of our basic business model:

- To focus on the development of people and provide a meaning and purpose for work
- To serve the recurring needs of customers, which generated recurring revenue and profits for a job well done
- To seek continuous improvement in the quality of the services delivered
- To provide channels of service close to the customer that would leverage the skills and commitment of the service provider and result in an efficient use of capital

This model resulted in maximum returns for our people, our customers, and our shareholders. As we grew our business, for every six cents we invested, we generated a dollar's worth of revenue and received back three cents in profits. There were times when we varied from this business model, and when we did so, we typically failed to live up to a standard of excellence for our people, our customers, and our shareholders.

The Two Unanswered Questions

As I mentioned earlier, when we came to the close of our SMIXX twenty-year planning period, we did so with two unanswered questions. One involved succession. The other involved the future direction and structure of our business.

Succession

At the beginning of 1994, my partner, Carlos Cantu, assumed the role of president and CEO of the company, while I continued to serve as chairman of the board of directors. Carlos had come to ServiceMaster as president of Terminix, and before his appointment as CEO, he had served as the leader of our consumer services business. He had a strong operating background and was doing a great job of leading the company when, early in 1999, he was diagnosed with stomach cancer. After several months of treatment, it became clear he would not be able to continue as CEO, and the board asked me to step back into that role.

The succession of leadership that built and grew ServiceMaster to become a star of the Fortune 500. (ServiceMaster photo. Used with permission.)

While there were other people in the company who had the potential to lead it, the board had some concerns about their readiness to do so. The board also wanted to take this opportunity to explore the possibility of hiring someone from the outside.

I agreed to come back and serve as CEO until my successor was identified and in place. I also advised the board that, in light of the second unanswered question that faced us, it was important to get the new CEO in place as soon as possible to participate in the decision process, because he or she would be responsible for its implementation.

Future Direction and Structure for the Business

For the future of our business and the continued growth in the value of our company, we needed to make a strategic decision about its direction and structure. It was my judgment that with our current direction and structure we could not maintain the growth in value creation we had achieved in the past. I felt we should either become an integrated operating company or a holding company with separate subsidiary units.

If we chose the integrated operating model, there would be substantial cost savings at the operating level that could be passed on in lower prices to the customer while also improving our bottom line. If we chose the holding company model, there would be cost savings coming from significant overhead reductions, but not to the same extent. However, the holding company model would give us more flexibility in adding new businesses and spinning off existing businesses to our shareholders, creating separate public companies and providing the potential of a new dimension of value.

I reminded the board of the advice Warren Buffett had given us several years earlier when he was still a shareholder of ServiceMaster. He told us that high growth rates eventually forge their own anchor, resulting in a negative effect on value unless a strategic change of structure or direction is made.

After several months of considering the issues before us, the board decided to initiate a process of selecting a new CEO, looking at both internal and external candidates. By the fall of 2000, an external candidate was selected, and we began 2001 with a new CEO. I agreed to continue at ServiceMaster in an advisory role for another twelve months and then retire from active involvement with the firm.

About six months into the job, the new CEO decided not to proceed with either one of these strategic directions for the business, both of which had been reviewed with the board, and determined that the company should sell its management services business and focus on consumer services—the business that he viewed as the growth engine of the future. I did not agree with his conclusions and felt they could have an adverse effect on the people and value of the company.

Five years later, with no appreciable growth in the value of the company, the board initiated an agreed-upon termination of his employment and appointed one of its own members as the next CEO of ServiceMaster, and then proceeded to sell the company to a private equity firm.

Businesses Are Built to Serve, Not to Last

The business firm is a market *vehicle* to profitably produce goods and services that customers need and want. I believe that in performing this function, its leaders should also be about crafting a culture of character with a focus on the care and development of the people who are producing the results of the firm. If a business firm no longer performs its basic function, in a free market there is no reason for its continued existence. It is a vehicle that has nowhere to go, nowhere to be driven. The business firm is not an institution to be worshipped.

As I write this book, the people of ServiceMaster are still providing quality services to customers. Although the original objectives of the firm, including "To Honor God in All We Do," have been changed, there are still many good people within the firm who are committed to accomplishing the intent and purpose of those objectives.

The history of ServiceMaster, with its successes and failures, is there to examine. For more than fifty years, the company was a vital market vehicle that was used by God to work in the lives of people as they served and contributed to others. Its legacy extends to those people still within the firm who have learned that in doing they were also becoming as they served others. It also extends to those people who are no longer part of the firm but who continue to reflect its original objectives and values as they contribute in other work environments and invest in the growth and development of people.

The legacy and example of ServiceMaster also extends to a growing number of people in business who are seeking to integrate the claims of their faith with the demands of their work.

The future of ServiceMaster is yet to be determined. Leadership will make the difference. As Drucker reminded us, "A leader has only one choice to make—to lead or mislead."

When the sails are full, it's time to steer for open water with a firm hand on the tiller.

Sailing into the Future

Planning is a tool for setting a course for the future. A plan provides a reference point for determining whether the changing winds and currents of the future will improve and enhance the agreed-upon course, or whether it is necessary to "come about" and change direction.

Planning is not just a process of determining a wish list of needs or wants. Instead, when done well, it encourages continuous learning, innovation, and preparing people for change. Whether we do planning for an organization or for ourselves, there is always the limitation of our temporal mind-set. But remember, God always plans with eternity in view. Therefore, the effect of our plans on the welfare of people and who they are becoming in this life and in the life beyond should always be our primary focus. In so doing, the question of God, His role in our lives, and His plans for the future cannot be ignored.

> We toss the coin, but it is the Lord Who controls its decision. (Proverbs 16:33, TLB)

8

The Reality and Responsibility of Authority

What life have you if you have not life together?
There is no life that is not in community
And no community not lived in the praise of God.

Can you keep the city that the Lord keeps not with you?
A thousand policemen directing the traffic
Cannot tell you why you come or where you go.

T. S. ELIOT

Whether we like it or not, all of life is lived in submission to some form of authority, and often that authority has the power to enable or restrict our freedom.

Authority implies a claim of legitimacy for the right to exercise control over the conduct of others. The common structures of authority in our society include parental authority in the family; corporate authority in schools, businesses, health care providers, and charitable organizations; and governmental authority in the community, state, and nation. These authority structures are not perfect. They can be wrong and make mistakes. They can add to the uncertainties of life. The reality for each of us is that there is much about living that is not in our control.

It starts at birth. We did not control when we were born, where we were born, our race or nationality, our gender, our family, or whether our parents were rich or poor. Any one of these factors can have a significant influence on the opportunities of life. None of us knows for certain how long we may live; neither can we predict what joys or sorrows may be ahead of us or what actions may be taken by government or others with authority that may have adverse effects on us or limit our choices in life.

So How Shall We Live?

As I reflect upon the uncertainties of life, I am reminded of a talk C. S. Lewis gave to first-year students at Oxford University in the fall of 1939. The title was "Learning in War-Time." That period of history was a time of great uncertainty. Germany had invaded and conquered Poland in a matter of weeks. Both France and England had declared war on Germany but were not prepared for war. America had stated it would stay out of the conflict. Germany's military strength was growing and the *blitzkrieg* was a terrifying reality.

In such a world, why were these students coming to learn the classics at Oxford University? What did Plato, Aristotle, or Shakespeare have to do with current events? As he posed these questions, Lewis reminded the students that the presence of evil and the violence of war really didn't change anything. All they did was aggravate the reality that there is much about life that is not in our control and at best is often uncertain. He then pointed out there were some things that were in their control, including the daily choices and opportunities they had to participate in the process of learning.

As Lewis concluded his talk, he emphasized that, as the students faced the uncertainty of life and realized all that was not in their control, they should take time to reflect upon Who was ultimately in control and their relationship to Him. Death was not the end of existence. There was a God to face, and the question for these students to answer was whether or not they had a relationship with Him.

War accentuates the uncertainties and incongruities of life. Over 150 years ago, Abraham Lincoln had to face these realities as our nation headed into a civil war, with both factions claiming God was on their side. Lincoln was personally opposed to slavery, as reflected in his debates with Sen. Stephen A. Douglas in the 1858 senatorial campaign in Illinois. However, as the president and leader of the country in 1861, his primary objective was to preserve the union. To do so, he had to accept the political compromise of containment, not the elimination of slavery. As a result, when the war broke out, he was able to keep the border states within the union.

At the same time, he was deeply troubled by the view expressed by the Supreme Court in the Dred Scott Decision of 1857, when the court concluded that a black slave was nothing more than chattel or a piece of property and had no protection or standing as a "person" under the Constitution.

As the pain of war grew in intensity and he suffered great disappointments in military leadership, Lincoln concluded that the real issue was not whether God was on his side but, as the leader of the nation, whether he was on God's side. How were his leadership and exercise of authority as president reflecting the true nature of God—a God Who had created every person in His image and likeness with dignity, worth, and the right to be free? As a result of these struggles, Lincoln issued the Emancipation Proclamation on January 1, 1863, and then pressed Congress for the adoption of the Thirteenth Amendment to the Constitution.

Learning God's Way

As a Christian, I want to be on God's side. As I have sought to understand and accept the reality of His ultimate authority in life, my faith has grown, and so has my ability to entrust the future to

Him. As part of my humanity, however, there continues to be the desire at times to be in control.

As I mature in my faith, I am learning that, when the desire to control begins to be consuming, I should step back and seek to learn what God is telling me so I may know His way.

The first time I can remember experiencing this desire was during my troubled teenage years. I wanted more control over my life and began resisting the authority of my parents, my school, and the God of my faith. During my freshman year in high school, I wanted to experience what my friends and I considered some of the pleasures of life, such as smoking and drinking beer.

My parents had determined I should go to a Christian high school that had restrictions against such activities. All students had to sign a pledge that they would not engage in those activities. I signed the pledge, but I ignored it and went along with my friends in seeking these forbidden pleasures. I worked hard at keeping it a secret from my parents and the school. The time came, however, when my secret became known. There was a price to pay. Those of us who were involved were put on probation. We had broken the rules and deserved to be punished. But it was done in a way that classified us as the "bad kids," without an acknowledgment that other students were doing the same thing. From then on, I kept my word not to smoke or drink, but as I did so, I developed contempt for how the school was imposing its authority.

I had a similar issue with the exercise of authority a year later at summer camp. I had grown up attending this camp since it had first opened. My father was one of the founders. There were many fun things to do at camp, but there were also chapels to attend twice a day. One hot morning, several of us skipped chapel and went for a swim in the lake. We found two other kids, not from the camp, on the pier. When one of them jumped into the deep water, it was obvious he did not know how to swim, and we dove in and saved him from drowning.

The lifeguard in the state park adjacent to the camp saw what was happening and came over to see if everything was all right. He praised us for what we had done. He asked whether we were from the camp, and we said we were. After the event, we were able to sneak back into camp without being noticed.

The next day, the head of the water-safety patrol came to the camp office to thank us and the camp for what we had done. When the camp director discovered what had occurred, he thanked the water-safety patrol for their interest and then sat down with us to determine what would be our punishment. He concluded that we needed to be punished in a public way to discourage others from doing the same thing. So, for the rest of the week, we had to wear armbands that said, "In disgrace." We broke the rules and needed to be penalized, but once again it was done in a way that I felt was an unfair exercise of authority.

These two incidents, along with some others later on in my high school career, fueled a growing contempt for authority and a desire to be in control of my life. They also had a chilling effect on my spiritual life. While I still believed in God, there was not much initiative on my part to develop a relationship with Him. I was avoiding it. Although I was developing a growing contempt for authority outside the home, it was never directed at my parents. I had learned to trust them. Although I was not always faithful, I had a desire to obey them.

There was one more experience at camp that became a major turning point for me. It was when I was eighteen and serving as a junior counselor. Near the end of my second week, God used a young boy to wake me up to His continuing love for me and His desire to have a closer relationship with me.

It was Thursday night and chapel was over. The boys were tired. After the senior counselor gave his devotional thought, they all went to their beds. As we came into the counselors' room, the senior counselor told me he was going to the kitchen for coffee and doughnuts, and I should look after the cabin until he got back.

Soon after he left, there was a knock on the door. I opened

it to find one of our boys with a sober look on his face. He said, "Counselor Bill, could you help me find Jesus?" As I invited him in and we sat on my bed, I found myself reading to him some of the same verses from the Bible my mother had read to me ten years earlier, when I was first seeking to find Jesus as my Savior. After I answered some of his questions, he prayed a simple prayer to ask forgiveness for his sins and accepted Jesus as his Savior. As he left, he thanked me, and in my heart, I thanked Him.

It was a transforming experience for both of us. God used it to show me that my kicking "against the pricks" of authority (Acts 9:5, KJV) was self-centered. I was focusing on me and what I wanted to do and control, not on Him and developing a growing relationship with Him, seeking to understand and know His way.

Learning to live my life seeking to know Him and to be known by Him has been an ongoing process. There is still much for me to learn. Sometimes I need a nudge from Him to remind me that life is not just about me. He is in control and knows the end from the beginning. These nudges come in many different ways, and at times they can reflect God's sense of humor as He gets the point across.

A Nudge on the Sixteenth Floor

One such nudge occurred as I was retiring the second time from my leadership responsibilities at ServiceMaster. During that period, I was also involved on the boards of several other public companies. As part of that involvement, I had to make a quick trip to New York for a board meeting early Monday morning, go on to Boston for an afternoon meeting, and return home that night to be ready to attend an important meeting the next morning at ServiceMaster. It was a very tight schedule. I had to be in control of my time if I was going to make all the meetings.

I arrived in New York on Sunday evening and checked into my hotel in midtown by nine o'clock After reviewing the materials for the meeting the next morning, I called Judy to say good night, then went to bed and had a good night's sleep.

I got a wake-up call at six o'clock the following morning so I would have plenty of time to take a shower, dress, and get to the breakfast board meeting by seven thirty. Before I took my shower, I decided to get the morning newspaper, which is usually right outside the door of the hotel room. I opened the door and saw the newspaper. It was not right next to the door but near the center of the hallway. When I stepped out to pick it up, the door of my room closed behind me.

There I was, at six thirty in the morning, in the middle of the hallway on the sixteenth floor in my pajama bottoms, without a key to get back into my room. I was not in control.

By this time, other hotel guests were coming down the hallway, heading to the elevator for breakfast. What was I going to do? The only thing I could do was follow them to the elevator so I could go down to the front desk and hopefully get another key to my room. Naturally, because of the way I was dressed, I was the focus of attention on the elevator as it stopped at six floors on the way down. All I could say in response to the stares was, "I got locked out of my room."

We finally arrived at the main floor. When I got out and walked across what was by then a busy lobby to the front desk, there were more stares and a round of laughter.

When I explained my predicament to the bewildered clerk behind the desk, she asked, "Do you have some identification?" I reminded her I was in my pajama bottoms and didn't have my wallet with me when I locked myself out of my room. She advised me that it was against hotel rules to give a key to someone without identification. Despite my circumstances, she was not going to make an exception to the "authority" of the rules. She told me to go back upstairs and wait in the hallway for a security man, who would let me into my room. She promised he would be there in fifteen to twenty minutes.

So once again I walked across the busy lobby to greet an elevator coming down full of people appropriately dressed for a workday in midtown Manhattan. As the elevator door opened, they were met by a man standing in his pajama bottoms. You can imagine their reaction and comments.

I finally got back up to the sixteenth floor and waited another thirty minutes for the security man to arrive—all the while trying to explain to the people walking by why I was standing there in my pajamas. By the time I got back into my room, took my shower, and got dressed, it was already seven thirty. I arrived late to the breakfast meeting.

The meeting went longer than expected and I missed my plane to Boston. I was able to catch another plane thirty minutes later, but as a result of the delay, I was more than an hour late to the meeting in Boston and missed most of the important discussions and actions taken. However, after that meeting was over, I was able, with only minutes to spare, to catch a later flight home that night so I could be at the meeting the next morning at ServiceMaster. Had I missed the flight home, I would have had to travel back to New York to follow up on some unfinished matters with several of the board members I had been with earlier that morning.

It was one of those days when not much seemed to go the way I had planned. I was not in control, and I also felt I was not very effective at the meetings I attended.

As I was traveling home that Monday night, reflecting on the events of the day and reading my Bible, I was reminded once again that God knows the beginning and the end. He knows the path of my life, and my steps are established by Him. Little did I realize then how His hand of protection was with me as I was able to catch the flight back to Chicago and not return to New York.

The next morning was September 11, 2001.

Authority in the Life of an Organization

What constitutes good governance and the proper exercise of authority for institutions? Are there certain principles to follow? As part of my life journey, I have had the opportunity to serve on the boards of directors of public and private business corporations, educational and health care organizations, charitable and religious institutions, and private foundations. In sharing some lessons from my experience, I do so not as an expert but as one who is still learning and who has felt the weight of responsibility and accountability that goes with the privilege of sitting at the table.

Mission

A meaningful mission for an organization is a statement of purpose that, when implemented, will provide a beneficial result and inspire people to collectively work together to accomplish that result.

As Peter Drucker often reminded us, "People work for a cause, not just for a living." As we found at ServiceMaster, a clearly stated mission provides more than a common cause. It also provides an ethic for the firm to encourage people to do what is right and avoid what is wrong. As people embrace a mission, one that provides a reason and purpose for their work and which also is in alignment with their own values, a powerful force is unleashed for innovative and productive results.

Mission and Good Governance

- Without a meaningful mission, an organization has no purpose for existence.
- Without effective implementation of that mission, an organization has failed and will soon cease to exist.
- Leadership and good governance are essential for the determination of a meaningful mission and for its effective implementation.
- Good governance is the product of an effective board.

The Effective Board:

- has qualified members who are committed to the mission of the organization
- knows and understands who owns this place, who runs this place, and who is responsible for this place

- has selected and supports a capable and committed leader and knows when to make a change
- understands its role in decision-making and its responsibility for oversight in anticipating a future that may have already happened
- has established a functional committee structure, a work plan, and a process for selecting and retiring members, appointing leadership, and conducting assessments of the performance of the board and its individual members
- is committed to the growth and development of those serving the organization and those receiving benefits from the organization
- is committed to the growth of the culture of the organization as a moral community for the development of human character

Serving as a member of the governance structure of an organization is a big job. It is time-consuming. The process of exercising authority over others never produces a neutral result. It is either effective or ineffective, positive or negative.

Qualification of Members
Drucker stated it very simply and directly: "The first requirement [of a board member] is competence." He suggested that, as part of that competence, there should be some experience and proven ability in serving as an executive of a business, governmental, or nonprofit organization. While this may be a good general standard for testing competency, I have found it is also important to have a variety of skill sets on a board. In my experience, doctors, lawyers, theologians, and, yes, mothers and homemakers can effectively serve as competent directors. It comes back to understanding the importance of the mission of the organization and the mix of skill sets needed to support and advise the leader of the organization. Every board needs some members with business experience to help develop and monitor a plan for meeting the financial needs of the organization.

Since the passage of the Sarbanes-Oxley legislation, most organizations are also focused on the importance of the independence of a director. While issues of conflict of interest or a potential conflict of interest have always been matters to be considered and disclosed, the requirement of "independence" suggests an even higher standard.

Unfortunately, there are several definitions of independence. The general purpose of the requirement, however, is clear: the independent director should have no relationships or other limitations that would in any way impede him or her from acting in the best interest of the organization. If a director has any such relationships or limits, he or she must disclose them and may not serve on certain committees of the board, such as the compensation or audit committees.

Often directors have developed social, professional, or even business relationships with each other that are external to the operations of the organization. While these relationships may not typically raise a "legal" independence question, at times they may be perceived to do so and may adversely affect actions by the CEO or by the board that would otherwise be in the best interest of the organization.

Such a situation occurred when I was serving on the board of trustees of Wheaton College. Several of us on the board were also connected with ServiceMaster. I was CEO of ServiceMaster, two other board members of Wheaton had previously served in that capacity, and two other members of the Wheaton board were serving as directors of ServiceMaster. In addition, the college had received large gifts of ServiceMaster stock, and the institution was benefitting from the growing and increased value of that stock.

Although we each acted independently as we came to serve on the college board, there was a perception among some of the faculty that there were too many ServiceMaster people on the board. As a result, a question was raised whether Wheaton could explore the benefits that might come from contracting with ServiceMaster for its plant operations and maintenance services. ServiceMaster had agreed to provide these services at a significant cost savings to the college and with no profit to ServiceMaster. However, perception, as it sometimes does, became a reality. In the judgment of the president, contracting directly with ServiceMaster could have a disruptive effect on the morale of some of the people in the organization and might limit the effectiveness of his leadership.

While I and the other directors connected with ServiceMaster were willing to step back from the Wheaton board so the college could receive the benefits of the contract, the other members of the board determined this would not be in the long-term interest of the college. To resolve the conflict, I decided to withdraw the ServiceMaster offer to serve. The exercise of authority in the governance of an organization can sometimes have imperfect results, even though all parties involved are fully committed to the mission of the organization.

Diversity

Some diversity among board members is important. Diversity of gender, race, and people with a global perspective will have a growing importance for many organizations. But diversity should never be sought at the expense of competency. Every director should be reminded that no individual director has the privilege of representing only a special group of people. Directors are to serve and represent all the owners or constituencies of the organization.

Who Owns This Place, Who Runs This Place, and Who Is Responsible for This Place?
Who Owns This Place?

For most business organizations, the answer to this question is the shareholder. This is the standard legal response. It was just such a response that the CEO and the board of ServiceMaster gave in

November 2006 when exploring a possible sale of the company. In a news release issued by the company, the CEO commented on his confidence in a bold business plan for the future that called for double-digit growth in earnings per share for the next year and mid-teen growth in earnings per share within two years, with cash from operations continuing to substantially exceed net income during this period. However, as he went on to comment on the company's exploration of a possible sale, he said that if such a transaction would produce a superior value for shareholders, the board would pursue the transaction.

The ultimate objective of the CEO and the board was clear. Their focus was to maximize short-term value for those viewed as the most important owners—the public institutional shareholders. But what about the other shareholders, including the owner-employees, who were in it for the long term?

In his book *Leadership Is an Art*, Max De Pree, former chairman and CEO of Herman Miller Inc., reminds us that the people producing the results of the firm—the people who have dedicated their working years to the firm and invested their lives and talents for the firm—are also important owners of the corporation. This corresponds with the view that I and my predecessors, as well as the boards we worked with, had as we recognized the ownership of the people of ServiceMaster. It motivated us to provide various vehicles through which they could also participate as shareholders of the firm.

For ServiceMaster, there were alternatives that could have satisfied both the short-term interest of the institutional shareholders and the long-term interests of others, including the people of the firm, but the alternatives would have involved more risk. Boards are often averse to risk. Were the added risks worth it? A judgment had to be made, and it was. There soon followed a sale of the entire company to a new owner.

All organizations, whether for-profit businesses or nonprofits, develop constituencies that benefit from and, in some cases, become dependent upon them. They are also owners. These include customers, students, patients, donors, and other people served by the organization.

Some faith-based organizations have a special view of ownership based on the teaching of Psalm 24:1. This passage reminds us that God, as the Creator, is the owner of all He has created. We are to be stewards over what we possess or manage, not owners. The two organizations I have worked with that most closely reflect this view are Wheaton College and the Billy Graham Evangelistic Association (BGEA). In both cases, the boards hold the belief that they have a fiduciary responsibility for the growth and development of the ministry of the organization. As such, they have assumed that awesome responsibility of stewardship.

Who Runs This Place?

The bylaws of most organizations stipulate that the organization shall be managed by the board of directors. In reality, it is the leader or CEO and his or her team who manage and run the organization. The major work of a board involves establishing policies, providing oversight, and making assessments. It is counterproductive for the board to get involved in management. The same is true for any well-intentioned individual board member.

The board must be prepared to support and give advice, but not to meddle or get in the way. The board members are not leading the organization but supporting the leader of the organization as he or she responds to the daily and long-term issues of implementation.

Who Is Responsible for This Place?

The board is ultimately responsible for the effective implementation of the mission. Board members work through the leader or CEO of the organization, but at the end of the day, the buck stops with them. *The board must assume the risk for doing whatever is necessary for the welfare of the organization.*

This principle is directly stated in the charter of Wheaton College, which in 1861 designated the board of trustees as a body politic and corporate by special act of the General Assembly of the state of Illinois.

Among the many provisions in this handwritten charter is a final charge to the trustees: "[To] do all business that may be necessary and appropriate to secure the permanency and prosperity of the College." Although this statement is more than 150 years old, in my judgment it is a good description of the ultimate responsibility of every board.

Another board I have had the privilege and responsibility to serve on that reflects a corporate responsibility with an eternal significance is that of the Billy Graham Evangelistic Association. For more than sixty-five years, this organization has had a single purpose: to proclaim the good news of the Gospel of Jesus Christ to a world of people who need to hear and have the opportunity to respond.

From the very beginning of this ministry, Billy Graham and his team were committed not only to preach the message of the Gospel, but also to live it. This commitment was reflected in a foundational document developed by Billy and his team, often referred to as the Modesto Manifesto. It set a standard of humility and love for their conduct with others; accountability and transparency in all things financial; chastity and discipline of life consistent with their faith and in support of their spouses and families; and integrity in their communications that reflects the truth of their words. These standards have become an integral part of the ministry.

As a board, we are responsible individually and corporately to be examples of supporting these standards in the governance and operation of the ministry. We were all reminded of this responsibility when Billy, for the fifty-seventh year, was recognized as one of the most admired people in America. The reputation of the man and the organization he founded provides credibility for a message and ministry that is of eternal value.

Selecting and Supporting the Leader

The selection and support of a capable and committed leader of the organization is *the* most important responsibility of a board. If a wrong choice is made, the board must subsequently make the painful decision to remove the leader. Both decisions are difficult. They require judgments to be made. There is a process that should be followed, but I know of no formula that will always assure success.

Periodic discussions about succession planning between the board and the existing leader are often a helpful preparation for a future selection decision. They provide a framework for the timing of the decision and the possible availability of internal candidates. During my years of service on various boards, I have been actively involved in the identification and selection of twelve CEOs. Based on that experience, I believe there is a better chance of success if an internal candidate can be chosen. Knowing the candidate over a period of years and having the experience of understanding his or her successes and failures, as well as his or her acceptance, or lack thereof, by the people of the organization, provides the edge for a successful selection and transition.

While search firms may be helpful in getting a broad view of external candidates and checking references, they are not always needed; neither can they provide the assurance of a successful selection. I have usually had a preference for selecting a person who had to be recruited over someone who was looking for a change or was primarily recruited by a search firm.

It is important during the interviewing process to ask direct and sometimes reflective questions. Some of the questions I often asked included:

- How do you determine whether something is right or wrong (seeking to determine whether the person has a moral compass)?
- Have you ever had to fire a person (seeking to determine whether the person has had the experience and pain of making this difficult management decision)?

- What are some of the books you are currently reading (seeking to determine the person's areas of intellectual pursuit)?
- What do you do in your spare time (seeking to determine how the person relaxes)?
- What are a few things you can tell me about your family life (seeking to learn about the person's relationships with family and others)?
- What is the most important decision you have made in life (seeking to determine whether the person will talk about the role of faith in his or her life)?

In three of the CEO selections I have participated in, the person hired subsequently failed. In each case, the board delayed too long in making the decision to remove the person, with a corresponding cost to the organization and its people. Unfortunately, this pattern of delaying a decision in the termination of a nonperforming CEO is not unique.

Two of the positive selections of CEOs involved Wheaton College and the Billy Graham Evangelistic Association. During Wheaton's more than 150 years, there have been only eight presidents. This result reflects a long history of God working through a board that is earnestly seeking His will in making the right decision "For Christ and His Kingdom" (the college's motto).

The BGEA has been in existence for more than sixty years and has had only two CEOs. The transition from Billy to his son Franklin occurred during a time when I was serving as chairman of the executive committee. It was clear from Franklin's experience in leading Samaritan's Purse that he had executive leadership ability. It was also clear from his service on the BGEA board and from his personal conversations with me that he was committed to evangelism and to the ministry and mission of the BGEA.

The board knew his style of leadership would be different from his father's and he would have an extended scope of responsibility, as he would serve as CEO of both the BGEA and Samaritan's

Purse. Since he has assumed both of these roles, he has done very well serving both.

In his leadership of the BGEA, he has initiated the move of its headquarters from Minneapolis to Charlotte and the establishment of the Billy Graham Library in Charlotte. He also has initiated changes in the ministry that have broadened the base of people to be reached by the Gospel, including establishing an Internet ministry and the My Hope ministry. Both of these ministries use new and developing technology to reach people in many different locations. Millions of people who might otherwise not have heard the good news of the Gospel have been touched. To date, as a result of these ministries, there have been more than seven million recorded decisions for Christ.

The Board's Role in Decision-Making, Oversight, and Establishment of Policies

Every decision has three dimensions: initiation, concurrence, and approval. One person may have the authority over all three of these dimensions. On the other hand, these dimensions of decision-making can be separated among two or more people or groups. With respect to the major decisions of an organization, it is important for the CEO and the board to have an understanding of their respective roles.

In most well-run organizations, the CEO has most of the initiating authority. The board's initiating authority is typically limited to the selection and removal of a CEO and to the compensation structure for a CEO. In both situations, the board usually has the responsibility for all three dimensions of decision-making.

Oversight is a very important function of an effective board. As Drucker often said, "A board is just as effective as the CEO wants it to be." If the board is not getting the right and necessary information about the operations and directions of the organization, its oversight will be ineffective. This is why it is important for the board to participate with the CEO in agenda planning that will cover several years and that will determine the items to be reviewed periodically.

As matters are presented to the board, it is also vital for individual members to scratch below the surface of the generalizations that are often included in reports, and to even ask some inconvenient questions. This is necessary, at times, to determine the depth of understanding of the presenter and the possible strategic issues that may be facing the organization in the implementation of what is being presented.

Such questions also provide for dialogue between the presenter and the board, and can be helpful in seeking a greater understanding of the implications of what is being presented.

Some people say I ask too many of these types of questions. When I was elected in 1999 as one of Corporate America's Outstanding Directors, the organization conducting research on nominees interviewed the CEOs of the various companies where I served on the boards and asked them for their views on my boardmanship. An article about the election process noted, "Pollard has an unusual knack for holding management to tough standards, while making its members feel valued." One of the CEOs interviewed was quoted as saying: "He does it in a unique fashion—and one that occasionally causes sleepless nights. . . . Management can't just wiggle away with a finessed answer."

Planning is an important function of the organization. The board has a role in the planning process and in approving the end result. Seeking to understand the current trends that will affect the future—a future that has already happened—often requires some education of the board. This type of education can usually be best organized by the chair of the board or by a lead director working with the CEO.

As part of understanding changes occurring inside and outside the organization that may affect its future, the board should continually look at what is happening at the margin or edges of the organization's operations.

Unfortunately, most of the statistics and financial information presented to a board are a compilation of averages. For example, a business board seldom looks at what is happening to the margin of profit or loss in the acquisition of new customers or a change in the retention rates of existing customers. A marginal revenue and cost curve tracing the performance of a product or a segment of the business is often helpful in determining a future direction that is already occurring.

The boards of educational institutions seldom look at what's happening at the margin of the debt levels of incoming students or the changing percentage of full-paying students. How does a board of an educational institution understand whether there is a margin of improvement in the learning process or whether there will be a marginal return in the quality of education from the expenditure of more capital?

Boards usually look at compensation in educational or charitable organizations using the average of a group, with years of service, not performance, being the primary basis for increases. The question of whether exceptional performers are being fairly paid is seldom reviewed or discussed.

As I close this section about the importance of asking inconvenient questions and looking at the margins in seeking to understand what we hear and see in oversight responsibilities, I am reminded of a lesson I learned many years ago in law school. It occurred in my evidence class at Northwestern, when we were discussing the role of cross examination in seeking to understand what an eyewitness to an event actually saw and heard. There were about one hundred students in the class, and it was held in a large auditorium with a stage in the front.

In the middle of our discussion, someone came screaming through the back door and ran down one of the aisles. This person was chased by another person with a gun. When the first person crossed the stage, the gun went off and the first person fell to the floor with what looked like blood on the person's chest. As the second person ran across the stage, there was a shout of some type of victory slogan, and then the person ran out the side door.

The professor helped the first person up and told us this was a staged event. He then asked us to describe what we had seen and heard. What did the assailant look like? What was said as the assailant crossed the stage? We discovered that some of us saw a tall person while others saw a short person; some saw a person with a black face while others saw a person with a white face. Most of us saw a person with long hair; some saw a woman and some saw a man. As to what we heard, some of us heard words with a Southern accent while others heard them with a foreign accent.

Did we know what we saw and heard, or did we see and hear what we already knew? We all saw and heard the same event. We all were eyewitnesses, but we described the event differently. Was it because our minds had conditioned us to see and hear based on what we had experienced in the past? Was our eyewitness experience tainted by our past experiences? A first impression is often worth testing to determine the true meaning of what is being said or done.

Organized to Work

Boards have a job to do. To be effective, they must be organized to do their work. Much of this work is done through committee structures. The standing committees of a board usually consist of a governance committee, a compensation committee, a finance committee, and an audit committee. There also should be an agreed-upon process of selection and a defined term of service for the officers of a board, which typically include a chairman, vice chairman, treasurer, and secretary. Terms of directors are generally limited to three years, although the Wheaton College board has effectively operated with terms of ten years.

Committee work is essential, but a board can also spend too much time listening to committee reports. As organizations grow more complicated, this is a tension point, and it often adds to the time board members have to sit through meetings. Some boards are increasingly using conference calls or Skype meetings to maximize the effective use of board members' time.

One of the key committees of a board is the compensation committee. The existing legal requirement for membership requires all members to be independent. For boards of business corporations, much has already been written about the excessive pay of CEOs and the unjustness of "golden parachute" provisions, especially when a CEO is fired for lack of performance.

The standards I sought to follow when I served on a compensation committee were similar to the standards we used at ServiceMaster. First, in a business corporation, it is important that the CEO and other senior officers have "skin in the game." They should have the opportunity to purchase (not just have options to purchase) a significant amount of company stock. The purchases should be made with the understanding that they will hold ownership of the stock as long as they are serving in senior executive roles. Also, their base pay should be below market standards and should be limited to an amount that is within a stated range above the lowest paid person in the firm. Incentive pay should be the major portion of their annual pay. It could be as high as three times the base pay if performance meets the target and zero if performance is less than fifteen percent of the target. Those who have more responsibility and have the opportunity to earn more should have more of their total pay "at risk."

For CEOs and senior executives of nonprofits, their base pay is typically a much higher portion of their total pay. There should also be an incentive package for their annual pay, as well as for a longer period of performance, such as three to five years.

Is there an optimum size for an effective board? Drucker often said to me that eleven to twelve is best. I've found that fifteen is a workable number. Wheaton College has operated effectively for more than 150 years with a twenty-person board.

Every board should have a defined method and process for the appraisal of the performance of the CEO, the performance of the board as a whole, and the performance of each board member. Tools are available to conduct all of these appraisals.

I have found that a "360" appraisal for the performance of individual members of the board is very effective in encouraging improvement in performance. It is also helpful in the rare case when a board has to ask for the resignation of one of its members. I have had to do this only twice. In both cases, the consistent view of other board members was the telling factor in achieving an orderly resignation.

Commitment to the Growth and Development of Those Serving and Those Being Served

An effective board must have a caring interest in the growth and development of the people within the organization who are making it happen every day. Are these people satisfied with their work environment? Do they see the job contributing to the person they are becoming? Would they recommend that their friends work for the organization? Has the level of satisfied employees decreased or increased? Are employee satisfaction and development used as measurements of the performance of the CEO and of the board?

Does the board spend time reviewing the training and educational programs for employees? What is happening to the turnover rates at various levels of the organization? If a layoff is necessary, does the board review how it will be conducted so that empathy and fairness are part of the process?

Can a board member dip within the organization without being disruptive to determine firsthand how people feel about their work? One way to do this is to be a customer of the firm.

An effective board also should be interested in the welfare of the people served by the firm, whether we call them customers, patients, or students. One of the joys I recently had in serving on the board of Central DuPage Hospital was seeing a significant improvement in patient satisfaction paralleling a corresponding

The Tides of Life

improvement in employee satisfaction and doctor satisfaction. I have found there is often a direct correlation between the satisfaction level of the person serving and the satisfaction level of the person being served. Boards should determine how they will regularly "touch" what is happening with the people serving and the people being served.

The Board and the Moral Tone of the Organization

Can a board be effective and not assume responsibility for the moral tone and action of the organization? How can an organization fulfill its mission and also be a moral community for the development of human character? Why shouldn't this be part of the mission of every organization?

Several months ago, I had a discussion with the director of a major financial institution regarding the causes of the recent financial collapse. I asked about the role banks played in packaging substandard mortgages into complicated securities that could be sold at face value and more because buyers did not understand the risk of what they were buying. As we discussed this issue, he kept coming back to the problems he was experiencing with the government regulations that had been imposed as a result of the economic collapse and the burden this was placing on the banks.

Continuing a discussion along these lines was not very constructive, so I came back to the way this complicated mortgage security was constructed and asked him a very simple question: "When your bank was packaging and selling these securities for a handsome profit, did anyone in the organization ask the question, 'Would I be a buyer of what I am selling?'" This was my way of putting the morality issue on the table. He became silent and then simply said, "No, I don't think so." As a director, wasn't he among those responsible for the moral standards and moral tone of the organization, so that the right questions would be asked as the bank was doing business and developing securities that could be sold to others?

Another example of a board's understanding and responsibility, or lack thereof, regarding the issue of the moral standards of a corporation involved Boeing. Several years ago, the CEO of Boeing resigned because he had been involved in an improper sexual relationship with a female employee. In announcing the resignation, the board chairman said the situation reflected poor judgment on the part of the CEO, and the board had concluded this would affect his ability to lead the company. The chairman then went on to make the specific point that this affair did not violate the company's code of conduct, although it may have hurt the company's reputation.

Given a statement like this about what is and is not immoral conduct, what is one to think about the board's understanding of morality and what is right and wrong? Didn't the affair reflect upon the integrity of the CEO's marital promise? Wasn't the affair an act of his deceit, a breach of his promise to his wife? Could she trust him in the future? Could the board and the employees of Boeing trust him in the future? You can't bifurcate moral standards. They apply to one's public or corporate life as well as one's personal life. In the absence of an absolute reference point or ultimate authority for determining a moral standard, there is no standard.

I believe the question of how an organization can fulfill its mission and also become a moral community should be on the agenda of the board of every organization, whether for-profit or nonprofit. It is a governance issue. Boards should not ignore their responsibility to deal with it.

Raising the issues of morality and the importance of having an ultimate authority for determining right and wrong also raises the question of how God's authority should be reflected in the operation of any organization or institution in our society. It is a question that cannot be ignored.

Where is the life we have lost in living?
Where is the wisdom we have lost in knowledge?
Where is the knowledge we have lost in information?

The Tides of Life

You have built well
Have you forgotten the cornerstone?
Talking of right relations of men
But not of relations of men to God.

T.S. ELIOT

Have you not known? Have you not heard?
The LORD is the everlasting God
The Creator of the ends of the earth.
He does not faint or grow weary;
His understanding is unsearchable. (Isaiah 40:28)

9

In My End Is
My Beginning

The title of this chapter is the concluding line in the poem "East Coker" by T. S. Eliot. Eliot begins the poem with a different emphasis as he says, "In my beginning is my end." Then, in superb poetic form, he reviews the reality, and sometimes frustration, of the many beginnings and endings that are part of this process of living. Here are a few more lines to provide a sense of the emotions one feels as he or she reads this classic poem:

In succession
Houses rise and fall, crumble and are extended,
Are removed, destroyed, restored, or in their place
Is an open field, or a factory, or a bypass.
Old stone to new building, old timber to new fires
Old fires to ashes and ashes to the earth . . .

Houses live and die:
There is a time for building
And a time for living and for generation . . .

Dawn points, and another day
Prepares for heat and silence. Out at sea the dawn wind
Wrinkles and slides. I am here
Or there, or elsewhere. In my beginning.

Old men ought to be explorers
Here and there does not matter
We must be still and still moving
Into another intensity
For a further union, a deeper communion . . .
In my end is my beginning.

Life's beginnings and endings involve relationships—relationships with family and with others, and the choice of whether we will have a relationship with God. Life also involves the toils and accomplishments of work, the joys and disappointments of serving, the pain and learning from failures, the grief and hope that come from the death of a friend or a loved one, the experience and challenge of continuous change, and the discoveries and limitations that come with growing older.

As I reflect upon the beginnings and endings of life and whether I have said anything of lasting value in this book, I am reminded of another poetic statement from the book of Ecclesiastes, where the author says in his concluding remarks, "Of making many books there is no end, and much study is a weariness of the flesh" (Ecclesiastes 12:12).

The book of Ecclesiastes is not an easy or quick read. There are times when the author seems to be making conflicting statements. I have found the writings of my friend Walt Kaiser and the sermons of my son Chip helpful in seeking to understand what is being said and taught. The author repeatedly reminds the reader that the inconsistencies, joys, and accomplishments of life, including wealth, pleasure, and the seeking of wisdom, are meaningless without an understanding of God's role in life and our relationship with Him.

God has given us the gift of time, and He provides us opportune times. He has created each of us with the freedom of choice—to fear, trust, know, and obey Him or to reject Him and seek to know and understand life without Him. The author of Ecclesiastes reminds us that consequences flow from choices. We are eternal beings whose existence does not end at death. In choosing to know and trust God and His ways, we look forward to that great hope of our faith, that at the end of this life there will be a new beginning with Him.

This hope is confirmed for those who choose to accept the redemptive work Jesus Christ accomplished as He lived among us, died, and rose again. Although we are unable to fully fathom all God has done and will do for us from the beginning to the end, we know that, "He has made everything beautiful in its time" (Ecclesiastes 3:11). Only God can fully understand the eternal significance of the joys, sorrows, and injustices of the present. His request for us in this life is to trust and obey.

As our relationship begins and grows with Him, we can have the assurance that with each end in this life there will be an opportunity of a new beginning:

Those who hope in the LORD
    will renew their strength.
They will soar on wings like eagles;
    they will run and not grow weary,
    they will walk and not be faint. (Isaiah 40:31, NIV)

What I have already written in this book reflects what I have experienced and learned from my relationships with God, my wife and family, my friends, and the colleagues I have worked with in the practice of law, serving in leadership and teaching at Wheaton College, and serving in the leadership of ServiceMaster.

Since completing my active involvement with ServiceMaster more than ten years ago, I have had many opportunities for new beginnings. These beginnings have involved placing a greater focus on nurturing relationships with family; continuing to foster and learn from relationships with existing friends and developing new ones; initiating a more active involvement and relationship with some of the Christian, charitable, and educational organizations we support; and making a renewed effort to engage and encourage business leaders to integrate the claims of their faith with the demands of their work and to recognize their responsibility to set a standard for the business firm to become a moral community for the development of human character. These new beginnings have involved change and the need of a readied mind to seize opportunities.

The Treasure Chest of Family

Judy and I started dating in high school and decided to get married five years later. It proved to be a great decision because of the commitment we made to each other and what we have done to fulfill that commitment. Great decisions in life are often like this.

The beginning of our life together.

We are two different personalities who love each other and who keep working at smoothing the rough edges. We have a common commitment of faith that extended to the raising of our children in the love and admonition of the Lord. Each of our four children later made that same commitment of faith.

Judy describes our marriage as a partnership of give and take.

There were times, especially during the ServiceMaster years, when I had a heavy travel schedule, that she kept the home fires burning with loving care for each of our children. She developed a special art of communicating with our children that always provided an open door for them to share the problems and joys of life. I found what is "good" when I found Judy, and I thank God for this blessing (Proverbs 18:22).

Our children, Julie, Chip, Brian, and Amy, have been a significant part of that blessing, and today they are mothers and fathers of their own children. They join me in praising and calling their mother blessed, one who is truly a Proverbs 31 wife and mother:

> Her children rise up and call her blessed;
>> her husband also, and he praises her.
> "Many women have done excellently,
>> but you surpass them all."
> Charm is deceitful, and beauty is vain,
>> But a woman who fears the Lord is to be praised.
>>> (Proverbs 31:28–30)

Several years ago, my children and I decided to write the following joint letter to my wife and their mother on Mother's Day:

To my bride, To our mother:

This is a special day, so says the world around us. It is Mother's Day. Too often we forget to express our appreciation for you, so someone has designated a day to remind us that mothers are important.

You are the best and we are ready to shout it from the housetops.

You are always there to listen, not just in a passive way, but as an active listener—sometimes overactive as you continue to ask questions in seeking to know and understand where we are.

You are always there to help with homework, typing, errands, rides, clothes, etc.

You are always there for words of advice and encourage-ment, seeking to match your wisdom with our moods and temperaments.

You are always there as an example of love, empathy, and special insight.

There is a word that helps us summarize all this, and it is "availability." You have always been available. Such availability does not just happen. It occurs because you have set a priority of serving your family.

How do you keep up with serving us all? It is only by and through God's grace and strength that such service is possible. We all love you very much.

Love from all of us

My new beginnings with Judy include more time together for travel, more sharing in the sporting and other experiences of our grandchildren, more understanding of each other as we continue to blend our differences, and more learning from each other as we share spiritual insights during our devotions together. More recently, she has encouraged me with her love for our extended family of the future as she has taken on the project of knitting baby blankets for our great-grandchildren yet to be born. She also has my enthusiastic support for one of her new beginnings, which involves developing her gift as an excellent artist.

A Heritage from the Lord

Our children, Julie, Chip, Brian, and Amy, represent a heritage from the Lord (Psalm 127:3). Each of them has chosen a partner for life, and the children from their unions now crown our life—an end result that will have many new beginnings. We have a heri-tage to pass on—the beliefs, customs, and convictions we received from our parents and grandparents. Each of our children brings a unique self and personality to the life of our family.

My daughter Julie has a gift of mercy, extending herself many times for the benefit of her children and for many others in need, including serving as a foster mom for over twenty-five babies waiting for adoption.

God has given Chip a bright mind. He has always been an avid reader. He is a great communicator and teacher in both the oral and written word. He is a leader who inspires people to follow. He is well suited for his present role as president of John Brown University, and, yes, he also has a tender heart committed to supporting and nurturing his children.

Our four children at a young age. They have been a heritage from the Lord.

Brian is transparent and his demeanor inspires trust. He has been successful in doing business as a real estate developer, and most of the time (except when he gets excited on the sidelines while coaching his basketball team) he is even-tempered. He has overcome some challenges in life and has a strong commitment to serve and nurture his family.

Amy is a faithful mother and wife. She has a servant's heart. She never looks for recognition but is always organizing and helping in the background to get the job done, and, yes, she even helps her father in the office, for which I am very grateful.

As our family has grown, Judy and I have been blessed with two sons-in-law, Chris and Mark, and two daughters-in-law, Carey and Becky. All of them have become part of the family, bringing his or her own special gifts and contributions.

The Crown of Our Life

We have also been blessed with fifteen grandchildren. As each grandchild has arrived, he or she has brought a new beginning and different dimension to our lives.

Julie and Chris have four girls. Heather is the oldest. She is a graduate of Wheaton College and is married to Dan Hawthorne, who is currently finishing his studies to become a doctor. Heather has a keen interest in serving others and has been working for a social service agency in Chicago.

Jillian received a nursing degree from Indiana Wesleyan University and is expressing her own gift of mercy as she serves children with special needs as a school nurse in a local school district.

Meghan is one of the star athletes of our family. She is just finishing her senior year at Wheaton College and is looking forward to what God has for her in the future.

Ali is also a fine athlete, with a high energy level that provides a spark to her personality. She is looking forward to finishing high school and then going on to college.

Chad is Chip and Carey's oldest son and, like his grandfather and father, he has now finished law school and is looking forward to pursuing a legal career. He has recently married his sweetheart, Anna, who is also Becky's sister. One of his unique roles in our family is that he is now both an uncle and a cousin to Brian's children.

As I mentioned in chapter 2, Chip and Carey's second son, Ben, passed away at the end of his junior year of college. There is a picture of Ben on the cover of this book when he was a young boy, sailing with his grandpa. Little did we both realize then that the course for his life would end at the young age of twenty and he would experience that blessed hope of our faith—being present with his Lord and Savior—before his grandpa. We miss him.

Our grandchildren have been the Crown of Life.

Emma is Chip and Carey's only girl. She is a smart and attractive young lady who is attending John Brown University and is following in the footsteps of her father as an English major and planning to pursue a teaching career.

James is also one of the star athletes in our family. He started on the varsity soccer team in his freshman year in high school and helped to lead the team to a state championship. As he continues his focus on excelling in soccer, he has also developed learning and leadership skills.

Jonathan is the oldest son of Mark and Amy. Like his cousin Meghan, he is finishing his senior year at Wheaton College. He is making plans for more school and a career in physical therapy. Jonny, as we call him, is athletic, bright, and winsome. He also has plans for marriage, and we all love Kirsten, who is soon to become his wife.

Abby is their second child and is also attending John Brown University. She is pursing a double major of art and psychology and hopes to use her skills and talents in a career of providing art therapy for special-needs children. Abby has always had a giving heart, as reflected in this letter I received from her when she was nine years old:

Dear Grandpa,

Thank you for the gift of $250 at Christmas. This is what I decided to do with the money. One, give half of it to Wheaton Christian Grammar School for families that need it. Two, give the other half to the College Church offering.

I decided to do this because I got everything I needed at Christmas and I wanted to share the money with others.

Thank you Grandpa for all the things you give to me and do for me.

Love, Abby—grandchild number eight

William is Amy and Mark's third child. Named after Grandpa, Will, like his cousin Ali, is finishing high school this year and plans to go to college. A good basketball and baseball player, Will is a person whom everybody likes. He is a team player with a focus on winning.

Maddy is Will's younger sister, and she is just finishing her freshman year in high school. She is an athlete, a good student, and also has a great gift for acting and singing. By far, she is the best singer in our family.

Brian and Becky's children are our three youngest grandchildren. Kaile is a beautiful, blond-haired little girl, quickly becoming a young lady. She is accomplished, smart, and knows her own mind. Grandpa appreciates her hugs.

Carson is a growing young boy and has a high energy level with a focused concentration on what he is doing. It is amazing what he can do with a computer.

Grey is the caboose of the family—both his family and our family. His smile is infectious. He is a boat lover and sailor like his grandpa. Our old wooden Chris-Craft is his favorite boat. His personality reflects that of his father.

Grandchildren are the crown of the aged. (Proverbs 17:6)

A Common Bond

As our children have matured, chosen life partners, and established their own families, and as our grandchildren are maturing and beginning to choose their life partners, we have become an extended family. Judy and I have attempted to provide an umbrella for this extended family, an umbrella that encourages the growth of each separate family unit, but also provides a common bond for the passing on of our heritage, which includes stories of family history, beliefs, customs, and convictions. One of the ways we have sought to do this is through the use of the family home in Lake Geneva.

Lake Geneva is a place with a long and rich history for us. Our involvement in the area started in 1894, when my grandparents, Thomas and Elizabeth Pollard (both emigrants from the British Isles), and their two children, Sadie and John, moved to Lake

Geneva. My grandfather took a position as farm manager for Mr. Chandler, who owned a large estate and a farm bordering the lake. Chandler later named the property on the lake Ceylon Court and the farm Ceylon Court Farm.

My father, Charles, was born on Ceylon Court Farm in 1897. When my father was ten or eleven years old, my grandfather moved the family to Chicago and started a business producing Pollard tea and coffee, an art he had learned in his younger years in London.

My father had good memories of his youth in Lake Geneva and returned there many times during his "growing up" years. After his return from World War I, he married my mother, Ruth. Our family grew to include three children—my two older sisters, Virginia and JoAnn, and me. Our family spent most of our summers at Lake Geneva.

After World War II, the property known as Ceylon Court Farm came up for sale. Although many of the buildings on the property were in poor condition and the previous owner had used most of the property as a chicken farm, my father had a vision for what it could become as a camp for boys and girls. He was a committed Christian who saw the use of this property as a way in which he could help children enjoy some of the same opportunities he had enjoyed at Lake Geneva while also learning of God's love for them.

The sale price of the property was $100,000. My dad asked four of his friends to join him in putting up $20,000 each for the creation of the Lake Geneva Foundation to purchase the property and operate the camp.

I was ten years old when the property was purchased, and I remember many times during that first summer walking over the grounds with my father as he shared his vision for its future and the use of its various buildings. This was a new beginning for him; a beginning that would become Lake Geneva Youth Camp and Conference Center. Over the next two years, volunteers from many churches in the Chicago and Milwaukee areas helped in refurbishing the buildings, and the first camp season was held in the summer of 1950.

Since then, the camp and conference ministry has grown and flourished, with contributions, input, and help from many faithful volunteers and staff. Currently, more than twenty thousand campers and guests use the facilities annually. The ministry has now grown to include another conference center on the lake, called Conference Point.

Over the years, most of our family, including my wife, my two sisters, their husbands, and our children, have been involved as campers, counselors, kitchen cooks, or members of the board of the Lake Geneva Foundation. It has become a part of the history of our family—a history and heritage that started with a new beginning more than a century ago, when my grandparents decided to move and raise their family on a farm in Lake Geneva, Wisconsin.

One Father's Day several years ago, I wrote a note to my children covering some of my thoughts on this idea of the common bond of the history and heritage of our family and how our memories and gatherings at Lake Geneva could not only support the separate identities and interests of each family unit, but also could provide an affirmation of a common mind and spirit regarding the essentials of our life and faith:

To my children,

It is Father's Day. Your mother and I have spent a good weekend together. Although I have not had the opportunity to be with each of you today, I do feel very close to each of you. Your presence is often more by mind than by sight.

Each of us has been created in God's image, including our body, soul, and spirit. It is through the mind that the spirit works. It is through our minds that our spirits commune with the Spirit of God. It is through our minds that our spirits commune with each other. It is the memories, the thoughts, the expectations of my mind that provide a closeness to each of you today.

As I do so, the memories of Lake Geneva and our times together as family there are cherished thoughts for me. Even though there have been some difficult times, including your mother and father being tight on the budget for fall school clothes, teaching you to swim by a forced jump at the end of the pier, imposing the rule of no TV, they were learning experiences for us and for you.

In seeking to be a father to you all, it is my hope that I have done more than just provided fish to eat but that you also have learned something about how to fish. I hope that each of you is refreshed and renewed from time to time in your mind and spirit as you reflect on your Lake Geneva experiences.

It has been and continues to be my expectation that the Lake Geneva experiences will be a unique way for you and your families to refresh and renew your minds and spirits and have the ability to commune and relate even though there may be differences and not always a physical presence.

It is also my hope and expectation that we, as an extended family, be of one mind and spirit on the essentials of our life and faith. The most important of these essentials is the commitment we have each made to have a relationship with God through our acceptance of the redemptive work of His Son, Jesus Christ. We pray and hope that all your children will also embrace this truth. It is a truth that has been part of the heritage of our family.

There are issues of life where we will not be of one mind. We will and should be different. We live in different houses. We work in different places with different occupations. We read different books. We have different interests. We have different abilities and personalities. We even raise children differently. As an extended family, we must continue to provide elbow room for differences. The more individuals involved, the more elbow room needed. Differences in nonessentials should not divide but instead enrich. We can all learn from each other.

Thanks for listening. My mind and spirit are with you. There is joy in knowing that there is nothing in between.

Love, Dad

On another Father's Day, I received this note from my son Chip:

Dear Dad,

Happy Father's Day. I wanted to write you a quick note of thanks. As you well know, it has been a long year and I feel as if I am just coming out of it. You and Mom have been a great source of encouragement and strength for us during the ups and downs. In particular, I deeply appreciate your unwavering confidence in me. It has helped to sustain me in some of the lonelier and discouraging times. I also appreciate your consistent prayers for me and my family. I can have the tendency to worry about things that I can't control, and it is a great encouragement to know that you and others are praying because it helps to remind me that I am not in control.

Your lessons of faith, love, and leadership have been interwoven into my life, and I am deeply grateful for that blessing. What Carey and I do in our work, church, and family here reflect the deep patterns of living and loving that we have learned from you and Mom. We just hope and pray that we can pass those lessons on to our kids.

So on this Father's Day, I just wanted to say thanks for being there. For being there as my coach in Little League when you told me to "bear down" to get the batter out (I just had to tell James yesterday to "bear down" and play in the basketball game even though his knee hurt). For being there to help support us through law school and as we are now doing for Chad. For being there when I did not have enough confidence in myself. For being there to ask questions and draw me out. For being there together throughout over fifty years of marriage as I hope to do with Carey. We love you dearly and wish you all of God's blessing on this Father's Day. We look forward to being with you in the next couple of weeks at the lake. All our love.

Chip and Carey and the kids

The Business of Family

As discussed in chapter 6, the words of Jesus about money, wealth, and possessions are clear and direct. Earthly possessions, including our time, talents, and whatever assets or wealth we may have acquired during our lives, have no eternal value unless they are invested and used for God's purposes. Profit as an end goal of life is an empty vessel and will result in the poverty of the soul.

God is the owner of all we possess (Psalm 24:1). He expects His followers to be faithful stewards and invest their possessions for returns that will have eternal value (Matthew 25:14–28). The growth and development of a family, including children and grandchildren, are a part of this stewardship responsibility. There is a "business of family" that involves a practical application of these stewardship principles and includes learning from successes and failures as we fulfill our responsibility to invest and produce.

Over the years, as Judy and I have reflected upon how we should implement these biblical principles, we have concluded that more than a majority of whatever assets or wealth we have acquired in life should be invested and contributed to charitable, educational, and religious organizations committed to doing God's work. The balance should go to our children and grandchildren. Our objective has been to accomplish these investments within our lifetimes, and we are now more than seventy percent there.

We created a family partnership called Fairwyn Investment and a family foundation called Fairwyn Fund to help in accomplishing this objective. We have involved our family in the decision-making process and sought to be an example for the stewardship and business of their families.

Learning from Relationships

The relationships we develop with other people become part of the process of defining who we are becoming. These relationships often start with acquaintances that develop into friendships.

Then there are special relationships of learning when the friend becomes a mentor.

Relationships at Work

Since we spend most of our waking hours at work, the people we become acquainted with, develop friendships with, and are mentored by in this environment often become an important part of our development process. This has been the case in all of my work environments and has been especially true with the friendships developed at ServiceMaster. Our culture at ServiceMaster was one that encouraged the mutual care and development of one another as we worked together under the banner of our four objectives.

The following note that I received from one of our leader/managers at the time of his retirement from ServiceMaster reflects this learning and supportive environment of our company.

Dear Bill:

I have been struggling and procrastinating about writing this letter because anything I say is inadequate in determining how I feel about our great company. I often think about the decision my wife and I made years ago to join ServiceMaster. When I left the sales job in Wisconsin, I had many friends who thought I had lost my mind. However, as Jean and I became aware of the objectives of our company, they were so in concert with what we believed and wanted for our lives that we took a step of faith. At the time, our children's ages were three and six. I can honestly say we never looked back or regretted the decision we made. I have had many challenging responsibilities over the years that have allowed me to grow as a person, to invest in others, and hopefully also to be used as a conduit by God to develop others.

Bill, you and others have given me opportunities that I never dreamed I was capable of doing. That confidence has meant more to me than I can ever express.

Jean and I will never forget all of the wonderful support for us when we went through Ann's illness and death. The call I received from you that Thursday morning in 1985, informing us that the executive committee had raised the age of insurance dependency, which allowed us the flexibility to place Ann in the proper nursing home, was one of the most incredible experiences of my life. I don't know if you know it or not, but Jean and I had our coats on when your call came in to begin our third straight day of searching for the nursing home that we would feel good about. Although this was approved by the board, I know it was initiated by you. Thank you.

Our corporate objectives have made it easy to keep our lives somewhat on track. I feel sorry for people who work for companies that require one standard for their personal lives and another for their corporate lives.

Bill, I thank you for your friendship and particularly for your leadership. Your vision for what ServiceMaster could become has and is becoming the reality, and your plan of action to accomplish this vision is what has enabled Jean and me to retire.

I have worked for some great people during my career, but I must tell you, Bill, that I consider Carlos as the "cream of the cream." His style of toughness with love, clear focus, and letting us run within the tracks has been a joy for me.

In conclusion, thank you for your very fulfilling career. Jean and I will always be leading the cheerleading team for our company.

Sincerely, Don

Friendships are fragile. When broken, they are difficult, and sometimes impossible, to put them back together.

One day, I was trying to emphasize this point with one of our executives, Brian Oxley, as he was about to assume a new leadership role in our company. I had concluded that, while he was listening, he was not concentrating on the importance of what I was saying. So I picked up a glass that was on my desk and threw it on the floor. It shattered into many pieces. I then asked him to pick up the pieces and put them back together. Of course, he could not, and he got the point of what I was saying.

A broken glass to illustrate the consequences of broken relationships. (Illustration by Brian Oxley. Used with permission.)

Brian continues to be a special friend. He is creative, intelligent, and often moves in many directions at once. He has a heart for people and a special love for the people of Japan. His parents were missionaries in Japan for more than fifty years, and he grew up there. Brian served in various leadership positions in our company, especially in our international division, and then assumed the role of a distributor for our businesses in Japan. He also became involved in an unrelated business in that market that soon developed a premium value and that he was subsequently able to sell.

He and his wife, Sally, continue to have a passion for serving the people of Japan, as reflected in the investments they made in northern Japan in response to the tragedy of the 2011 tsunami. He has also developed his gift of writing and has already published one book, *The Last Tower*, and is now working on another. Over the years, Brian and I have learned from each other. I am thankful for our friendship and for the way God has worked in his life as he continues to serve others as part of his passion to serve God.

One of the joys I have had in these years after my active role in ServiceMaster is to see how friends who served with me and contributed to my growth and development as we worked together in the company have not only continued as friends but have also developed their own new beginnings and are making significant contributions to the growth and development of others.

One way I keep in contact with many of these friends is to send them notes on their birthdays. As I write this chapter, I have just sent such a note to Ken Hooten. I first got to know Ken as a young boy who was a friend of my son when they were in grade school together. Ken came to America as an orphan from South Korea and was adopted by a loving family in our hometown. As he grew, he excelled in high school and college, and earned an MBA at Northwestern. He developed a career in real estate. It was then that I was able to recruit him to join the ServiceMaster team to lead an initiative of creating a company-owned venture fund for investing in new businesses that were marrying technology with the delivery of service. Ken was very successful in this assignment. We learned from each other. After my retirement from ServiceMaster, he left the company and initiated his own venture fund. I have had the joy of seeing him grow not only in business but also in his faith and as a husband and father of four children. His sensitivity and care for others has been an inspiration for me.

Relationships with Others

My relationships and friendships apart from my daily work environment have also contributed to my learning and development. In mentioning a few of these "others," I do so only as examples of the many friends who have contributed to my life.

For many years, Brian and Rachel Griffiths have been good friends of ours. The way they work together and support each other, especially in Brian's various leadership roles, has been a great example for Judy and me. Brian was a ServiceMaster board member during my years as CEO and chairman. He also served with me on the Herman Miller board. He currently serves as vice chairman of Goldman Sachs International in London and is also a member of the House of Lords. He has been an encourager, adviser, and, in his own way, a mentor to me. He has been able to engage people serving in the highest levels of his society, whether in government, business, or the academy, with the reality and truth of his Christian faith. We continue to work on several ministry projects together, including the Business School of Emanuel University in Oradea, Romania, and the Centre for Enterprise, Markets, and Ethics at Oxford, England.

Lord Brian Griffiths, a special friend who served on the board of directors of ServiceMaster and who gave one of our Hansen-Wessner Lectures on Business Ethics at Oxford. (ServiceMaster photo. Used with permission.)

Jerry Hawthorne was a professor of Greek at Wheaton College and a special friend for many years before he passed away in August

2010. He was my teacher, although I was never in his classroom. My spiritual growth was enriched by his thoughtful understanding of God's Word and its application to the issues of life. There was an integrity in his approach to the interpretation of the Bible that refused to avoid the difficulties and ambiguities of our faith. He always came back to the reality that God's love as exemplified in the redemptive work of His Son Jesus Christ was a truth that could not be ignored. We miss him and are thankful for our continued friendship with his wife, Jane, and for the privilege of getting to know his grandson Daniel, who became a part of our extended family when he married our granddaughter Heather.

Howard Matson is another one of those special friends who has been a spiritual mentor. He has dedicated himself to serving others as a pastor and shepherd. His life has truly been a testimony of what he believes, especially during recent years, when he has struggled with health issues, including a lung transplant. Despite the difficulties of life, he continues to reflect the joy and peace of God, and has been an inspiration to me. So has my brother-in-law, George Toles, who, despite the limitations of Parkinson's disease, has established an effective and meaningful ministry among business leaders in Seattle called "His Deal."

For many years, Joe Maciariello has been the Horton Professor of Management at the Peter F. Drucker and Masatoshi Ito Graduate School of Management at Claremont Graduate University. Joe worked closely with Peter Drucker when Peter was still teaching and writing. He knows and understands more about Drucker and his teachings and writings than any other scholar in the world.

Over the years, we have developed a close friendship. Joe and I have learned from each other. He studied and wrote about the ServiceMaster culture when I was leading the company. Since then, we have had many lengthy discussions about Peter's views of life, faith, the role of organizations, and their management. Some of our most intense discussions have been about Peter's concept of management as a liberal art. With a bit of nudging and support from me, Joe agreed to write a best-selling book about it with his colleague Karen Linkletter, entitled *Drucker's Lost Art of Management*.

Jim Heskett is another academic leader whose involvement and friendship have always resulted in learning experiences. Jim is currently serving as the Baker Foundation Professor Emeritus of the Harvard Business School. During my leadership years at ServiceMaster, Jim chose our company as the subject for several case studies taught at Harvard. He was intrigued by what we were doing in developing people as we served customers and sought to honor God as we grew profitably. He concluded that in so doing we were breaking the cycle of failure for the service worker.

Jim and his students taught me as he allowed me to participate in the classes when our case studies were being taught. From time to time, he would also advise our management team and board of directors. He has recently authored an excellent book entitled *The Culture Cycle*. As I look back and reflect, I wish we at ServiceMaster would have followed more of his advice.

Ming Lo Shao is a dear friend. He is a very successful Chinese businessman. He and his wife, Eva, have a passion for the people of China and have made a major commitment to give back to their countrymen.

I first met Ming Lo when he became our ServiceMaster partner in China. I later had the opportunity to introduce him to Drucker, and they developed a strong friendship. As a result of that friendship, Drucker gave Ming Lo permission to establish Drucker Academies in China, teaching Drucker management principles to a growing number of leaders. Today there are Drucker Academies in more than twenty Chinese cities, and over the last ten years more than twelve thousand people have participated in the learning process conducted by these academies.

Ming Lo and his team have been focused and persistent in accomplishing these results. I have had the opportunity to participate in teaching at some of the management seminars conducted by the Drucker Academies and have seen firsthand what is being accomplished in China. Ming Lo has taught me as he has taken an idea and then created something of significance and value. He is a great example of an entrepreneur with a servant's heart and a focus on results. I continue to learn from him as I now have the privilege of serving on the board of directors of the Bright China Foundation and the California Institute of Advanced Management, which is another of his new educational initiatives.

Ming Lo Shao and his wife, Eva, are committed to the teaching and development of people in China.

Don Soderquist is my brother-in-law and my friend. We both had careers serving in the leadership of public companies that were committed to growth. He had a much bigger challenge of size, as he became vice chairman and chief operating officer of Walmart. For many years, he participated with Sam Walton and others in leading and achieving extraordinary growth. After his retirement, he founded the Soderquist Center for Leadership & Ethics at John Brown University and is now active in its various leadership and training programs. Don and I have different styles, but we often think alike about how to address problems and resolve issues. We have learned from each other, and I have been inspired by the way he has planned and implemented his "new beginning" after Walmart.

There are two other faithful friends I would like to mention who have influenced my growth and development. My friendship with one began in high school and with the other in college. We have lived and raised our families in the same town. Dick Lauber and Dick Gieser, each in his own way, have been a continuing encouragement to me. They have always been available when I needed advice, and their responses have always been open, frank, and considerate.

As I come to the close of these reflections on the importance of relationships and friendships, I am reminded of the words of Proverbs 18:24: "There is a friend who sticks closer than a brother." I also think of the words of Jesus in John 15:14–15, when He said: "You are My friends if you do what I command you. No longer do I call you servants, for the servant does not know what his master is doing; but I have called you friends, for all that I have heard from My Father I have made known to you." What an awesome thought. As we follow God's ways, He becomes our Friend, and we begin to develop a relationship that will last beyond this life. My relationships with others have helped me begin to understand the significance of this relationship with God.

One of those special relationships that has contributed much to this understanding has been my friendship with Billy Graham. He has been not only a friend but also a mentor.

Our relationship began while I was serving in the administration of Wheaton College and he was serving on the board of trustees of the college. It continued when he asked me, soon after I joined ServiceMaster, if I would join the board of the Billy Graham Evangelistic Association. Then, after I had served on the board for several years, he asked me if I would consider serving as chairman of its executive committee. Several years after I accepted that role, we proceeded with the transition of leadership from Billy to his son Franklin.

Words of wisdom and advice from Billy Graham, whose life has been a consistent witness for the God he loves.

While these are some specific points of reference, they do not speak to the heart of our friendship. Over this period of time, there developed confidence, trust, and understanding in our communications with each other as we shared matters together and prayed about issues as only friends who trust each other can do.

The conduct, integrity, and spirituality of Billy's private life are consistent with his message from the platform. He and Ruth were partners in their marriage and in their desire to serve the God they loved. They both had a keen interest in Judy and me and our family. Ruth also took a special interest in my desire for ServiceMaster to do business in China and gave me some very helpful suggestions, books, and other materials on the country and the people.

Although Billy may not have thought of himself as a mentor of mine, he was one. I learned from him as I observed how he approached the process of decision-making, the conduct and authority of the board, the nurture and development of people, transparency in all things financial, and planning for the future, which included his initiation and preparation for a transition of leadership.

A special privilege of sharing a birthday party with Billy and Ruth at the White House. (Official White House photo. Used with permission.)

During the time of transition, he made it clear he was relying upon me, as chairman of the executive committee, to help in guiding the transition and making it as smooth as possible. He put it this way: "Bill, I want you to bridge the gaps and to make bridges of harmony when there is conflict, with always a spiritual perspective and point of view." As I have reflected upon his words, I realize they were descriptive of one of his great strengths of leadership. Other strengths were his humility and his constant suppression of any hubris, always giving glory and praise to God for the work He has done and will do. This mind-set has been an important part of the disciplined life of Billy Graham.

As I mentioned earlier, there was never a time when I met with him, in his office, home, hotel room, or hospital room, when there wasn't an open Bible that he had been recently reading, and either before or after our conversation we would have a time of prayer.

I will always be thankful to the Lord for the opportunity to serve Billy, Franklin, Cliff Barrows, Bev Shea, and other members of the BGEA team and those in the organization, who have dedicated themselves to proclaiming the good news of the Gospel of Jesus Christ.

Beyond the Bottom Line

Over the years, Judy and I have enjoyed engaging with and supporting people and the organizations in which they serve, as they seek to meet the needs of people who are in crisis or who live in developing countries of the world.

Recently, we traveled with most of our family to Guatemala. The primary purpose was to participate in the dedication of a new grade school named Ray of Hope. This school was constructed for children living with their families in one-room metal huts in one of the areas surrounding Guatemala City's garbage dump. The previous school had been a rented room in an old building.

Two years earlier, our grandson, Ben, and his father, Chip, had visited the old school and had been overwhelmed with the compassion of those teaching and caring for the students and the limited accommodations for the children. During the intervening years, the new school had been constructed with the help of many people, including the members of a church in America, and a portion of it was now being dedicated in Ben's memory. It was a moving experience for all of us.

We also had the opportunity to visit several other ministries working with the poor in Guatemala City. It was a special privilege and learning experience for us as a family to engage and encourage those dedicated people who were focused on serving those in great need.

Two other organizations that our family has been involved with are Samaritan's Purse and Opportunity International.

Operation Christmas Child, one of Samaritan's Purse's initiatives, recently celebrated the distribution of more than one hundred million shoeboxes to needy children all over the world. Another major ministry of Samaritan's Purse is its relief work of providing food, medical supplies, and temporary housing for victims of conflicts, wars, and natural disasters. It also has a ministry of supporting mission hospitals in underdeveloped areas of the world.

As it seeks to meet the physical needs of people, Samaritan's Purse is also committed to providing God's answer to their spiritual needs. Franklin Graham has led this organization with a passion to be an ambassador for Christ and to share the joy of His redemptive love to those the ministry serves.

Opportunity International—"Giving the working poor a chance"—is a provider of microfinance, supportive training, and counseling for the poor in more than twenty countries. The average loan is $150 to $300, and the organization's total client base has topped five million people. More than ninety percent of the borrowers are women.

I have had several opportunities to travel in African countries such as Sudan, Kenya, Uganda, and Tanzania, along with some of my children and grandchildren, to visit those benefitting from these ministries. While we found people living in desperate situations, we also found people with a hope for the future because others cared for their physical and spiritual welfare.

Additional areas of support and service include Emanuel University in Romania, Daystar University in Kenya, and Indiana Wesleyan University's International Business Education distance-learning program for students in developing countries; helping to establish and serve a new foundation in my home state of Illinois that is committed to supporting the health care needs of children; and serving on the board and as the chair of Central DuPage Hospital as we merged with Delnor Hospital to form Cadence, a new hospital system for the provision of health care in the western suburbs of Chicago.

Also, as part of my new beginnings, I have had the opportunity to return to teaching a course of business law at Wheaton College and to serve on the advisory board of the J. Dennis Hastert Center for Economics, Government, and Public Policy at the college. One of my joys in continuing to work with the college is to see two of my friends and team members at ServiceMaster, Steve Preston and Jim Goetz, now serving on Wheaton's board of trustees. Steve's leadership responsibilities after ServiceMaster included joining President Bush's administration as head of the Small Business Administration and then as secretary of the Department of Housing and Urban Development. Jim, who was our CIO at ServiceMaster, is now president and COO of Alta Resources.

Another initiative includes working with some of my other good friends from ServiceMaster, including Mike Isakson, Rob Keith, Ernie Mrozek, Dave Baseler, Brian Oxley, and two very successful franchisees of ServiceMaster, Tom Little and Bob Smith, in developing and growing an organization we call Delta One Leadership Institute. Its mission involves providing a values-based training and educational program for franchisees and their employees based upon what we have all learned and experienced in our ServiceMaster careers.

A Passion for People and Morality in the Marketplace

Since leaving my active role at ServiceMaster, I have had a growing interest in encouraging people of faith to integrate the claims of their faith with the demands of their work. I also have a passion to help business leaders recognize that the doing of business should include developing the "whole" person who is producing the results, and that the mission of the firm should include becoming a moral community for the development of human character.

During the last several years, I have used my opportunities to speak and write to encourage and inspire a greater implementation of these objectives that are very close to my heart.

Business as a Calling

As discussed in chapter 3, the topic of work as a calling for Christians is not new. However, the suggestion that the doing of business, the making of money, and the producing of needed goods and services for a profit is a calling, a ministry, or, yes, even a full-time Christian ministry is rarely discussed or taught in our churches. There has been some progress in considering this subject at the seminary level, helping future pastors and leaders understand all that is involved, and the Kern Foundation has done an admirable job in encouraging this process.

There are now more than one thousand parachurch organizations in America seeking to support Christians who desire to integrate their faith with their work. While the church is the logical "channel of distribution" for accomplishing this result, it is still mostly silent on the subject. People need to learn how to raise the question of God at work and to affirm their faith without imposing it.

Several years ago, I helped organize a consultation among ten Christian business leaders and ten church leaders on this subject. The consultation was held at the Billy Graham Training Center at The Cove in Asheville, North Carolina. We thought this would be an appropriate place to hold such a consultation since Billy had already suggested that the marketplace may be one of the greatest untapped mission fields in the world.

The consultation lasted two and a half days. There was open and healthy discussion. We agreed upon a summary statement that included the following conclusions:

Service to God in the Marketplace

Our Task:
To understand, practice, and teach
a biblical view of ministry in the marketplace

God created people *for* work and work *for* people. Our work can be a "calling" in doing God's work and a form of worship as we do it well and serve to develop others.

A biblical view of business includes business as a vehicle and a ministry to provide productive work in producing the necessary goods and services for an ordered society; to engage the diversity of people and their beliefs with the redemptive message of God's love and hope of salvation; to understand God's economy of surplus and learn His purpose for the use of profit and a return on the investment of our lives.

A biblical view of wealth includes God's purposes for wealth, our responsibility of stewardship, and knowing and resisting the pitfalls of wealth as an end goal of life.

The church needs to support those who serve God in the marketplace and recognize the importance of business as a calling and the workplace as a venue for ministry; resist the twin dangers of viewing those who work in business merely as sources of revenue and giving special treatment to the wealthy; and recognize the marketplace as an important mission field and equip those who work there for their witness.

The consultation was not a public affair and there has been little effort to publicize it. However, I believe its conclusions should be promoted. Recent encouragements include the work of the Kern Foundation; David Miller's book *God at Work: The History and Promise of the Faith at Work Movement* and his work at Princeton University; the book *Drucker's Lost Art of Management*; and leadership examples such as Dan Cathy of Chick-fil-A, John Tyson of Tyson Foods, and Frank Harrison at Coca-Cola Bottling Co. Consolidated.

The Business Firm as a Moral Community

Improving ethical behavior in the conduct of business should be a major concern of our society. This is not just because of the recent economic collapse, due in part to failures of ethical behavior, but also because of the inherent temptation of greed and the accumulation of personal wealth and power at the expense of others.

We need our business schools and leaders to recognize that the development of character is an essential part of the way we should conduct business. This is at the heart of what Peter Drucker was talking about in his concept of management as a liberal art.

As a discipline, management has allowed us to convert knowledge into a capital resource. As a discipline, it is involved in the development of various organizational structures, procedures, methods, and systems for getting the right things done through the combined efforts of people with a diversity of knowledge, skills, and talents.

Peter Drucker was a person who knew how to ask the profound questions of work and of life, such as "What is your business?" and "What is your priority?"

Drucker has reminded us, however, that as a discipline, management is also a liberal art because it is about the management of people, not just things. Every organization is a human community. Therefore, the effective manager should seek an understanding of the human condition that recognizes there is a spiritual dimension of our humanity that contributes to character development.

In giving advice to leaders of both for-profit and nonprofit organizations, Drucker often began by asking, "What is your business?" His purpose was not just to understand what the organization did and whether it was effective in so doing, but also to determine whether its leaders understood their responsibility for the growth and development of the people producing the results. It was one of his ways of introducing the subject of management as a liberal art.

Drucker suggested that to understand the human condition, one needed to draw upon the knowledge and insights of the humanities and social sciences, such as psychology, philosophy, economics, history, and ethics. If managers and leaders were serious about developing the whole person, they should know and understand their source of moral authority and a purpose and meaning for life and work. For Drucker, people were not just biological or physiological beings, but also spiritual beings who were created and existed for a purpose.

The following summary represents my learning from Drucker about the importance of understanding the nature of our human condition:

1. The uniqueness and value of people should be cherished and honored. Every person, regardless of status or position, has dignity and worth and a unique fingerprint of potential.

2. People have the freedom to make certain choices in life, including how they will live, what they will do with their time, and how they will relate to others.

3. People are imperfect in the exercise of their freedom to choose. They can make good choices and wrong or harmful ones. Although free to make choices, people are not free from the consequences of their choices or the responsibility for their actions.

4. Responsible people will be guided by a sense of humility and accountability to the will of a higher moral authority and will also be aware of their own imperfections.

Drucker recognized that this concept of management as a liberal art and its focus on the nature of the human condition, including its spiritual dimension as a source of character development, raised the question of God. It is a question that we must address as we seek a source for our moral authority. Although Drucker was optimistic about human potential, he was also realistic about human fallibility in such things as pettiness, greed, vanity, and lust for power.

Although the practice of management as a liberal art raises the question of God and the need for a personal response, Drucker would also say that in light of the differences in cultures, beliefs, and freedom of choice, it could not demand a uniform response, but also could not be ignored.

Management as a liberal art requires moral leadership; therefore, leaders and managers must:

1. Know and understand what is their source of authority for determining moral behavior
2. Know what they believe and why they believe it
3. Know where they are headed and why it is important for people to follow
4. Be examples of right behavior in their private and public lives
5. Be willing to walk in the shoes of those they lead
6. Help and guide people to find a sense of purpose and meaning in their work, a commitment to truth, and a strong ethic that extends to the care and service of others

When management is practiced as a liberal art, the work environment becomes a catalyst for innovation, respect, and performance that often exceeds expectations. This was our grand experiment at ServiceMaster.

My End Is My Beginning

For my children and my grandchildren, and others who may be reading this book, I now come to the end. But the end continues to be a beginning in this life until there comes that appointed day when my life is over and the opportunity of another new beginning and a different flood tide of life that will take my soul and spirit to a new Home, a safe harbor with my Lord and Savior.

> He made the storm be still,
>   and the waves of the sea were hushed.
> Then they were glad that the waters were quiet
>   and he brought them to their desired haven.
>   (Psalm 107:29–30)

Until then, there is work to be done, gaps to be bridged, and bridges to be built.

> An old man, going a lone highway,
> came at the evening, cold and gray,
> to a chasm vast and deep and wide,
> through which was flowing a sullen tide.
> The old man crossed in the twilight dim,
> the sullen stream had no fear for him;
> but he turned when safe on the other side
> and built a bridge to span the tide.
> "Old man," said a fellow pilgrim near,
> "you are wasting your strength with building here;
> your journey will end with the ending day,
> you never again will pass this way;
> you've crossed the chasm deep and wide,
> why build you this bridge at evening tide?"
> The builder lifted his old gray head—
> "good friend, in the path I have come," he said,
> "there followeth after me today,
> a youth whose feet must pass this way;
> this chasm that has been naught to me
> to that fair-haired youth may a pitfall be;
> he, too, must cross in the twilight dim—
> good friend, I am building this bridge for him."

WILL ALLEN DROMGOOLE

Judy has been a great partner in life and has helped me to keep an eagle eye on the Author of our faith. (Painting by Judy Pollard)

Afterword

By Chip Pollard

In the spring of 2004, John Brown University asked me to serve as its seventh president. I was an unconventional choice in many ways. I was just forty years old and was teaching in the English department at Calvin College. While I had a solid academic record, I had never served in academic administration, not even as the chair of a department, and neither had I had any other formal management role in my working life. It was not surprising, then, that there was some conversation on campus about my lack of leadership experience when I was appointed.

However, no one addressed it with me directly until I had a conversation with Dr. Richard C. Chewning. Dr. Chewning had retired as the emeritus Chavanee Professor of Christian Ethics in Business at Baylor University and was serving as the distinguished scholar in residence at John Brown University, working on scholarly projects and mentoring business faculty and students. He had met my dad in a variety of professional contexts, most notably through the Christian Business Faculty Association.

Dr. Chewning made an appointment and came to my office. He is a tall, gracious person with a deep, resonant voice. He congratulated me on being selected and reminded me of his relationship with my father. Then he said: "I know that some folks are worried about your lack of experience, and you will certainly have a lot to learn in this new job, but I just tell them that I know your father so I know a bit about the dining room table around which you grew up and about the conversations that you must have had at that table. You will do just fine." It was a vote of confidence that deeply encouraged me in those first few months.

He was right that I relied heavily on those stories I had grown up hearing, many of which are recalled in this book, as I thought about leadership, management, family, and faith in my first few years at JBU. I realized that you do not inherit leadership gifts as you might inherit genetic traits, and neither does the success of the father guarantee the success of the son; however, I do consider it a great gift that many of the principles outlined in this book were part of my leadership "instincts."

It has been a joy for me to implement some of those principles into my own context and trace the family legacy. So when I read again my dad's words about the importance of each person's contribution to the organization, it reminds me of why it is important in the annual president's report to recognize the gifts of both our grounds crew and our top scholars. When I read about the importance of staying close to the "customer," I think about all that I learn from students by continuing to teach a class or the question-and-answer time that I have with prospective parents. When he quotes Peter Drucker, as he does often, about defining the organization's results, implementing abandonment, or piloting new initiatives, I recognize the family legacy of some of the principles in JBU's most recent strategic plan.

Of course, it is not only in the business side of life that I see the echo of his insights. Work and family were always intermixed in our lives, not in some perfect ideal of "work/family" balance that is so often discussed in church or at work, but more in a sense of mutual and overlapping encroachment. I grew up in a family in which family responsibilities sometimes encroached on work and work sometimes encroached on family. Indeed, we used to joke in our family that Federal Express knew the itineraries of our family vacations because it always seemed to deliver a package to our hotel before we arrived. However, family time also encroached on work. I always knew that, if I wanted to get hold of my dad at work, he would interrupt a meeting to talk with me. I also knew that he arranged his travel schedule around my basketball games and that he and my mother were intensely interested in my life, asking questions and opening up conversations whenever and wherever possible. I knew that my parents were committed to work through the inevitable scheduling struggles of a busy career and family life, even though it was not always easy. Carey and I have similar conversations now, and we seek to compromise and prioritize our various family and work responsibilities.

We live in a broken world, so our family legacy is not all sweetness and light. My dad and I have had the normal conflicts of fathers and sons. Moreover, there are some characteristics of leadership that I may have absorbed from him that are not always productive. I don't always listen as well as I could before making a decision. I can ask questions in a way that gets to the heart of an issue but that may hurt the confidence of a person. When I am stretched by stress or busyness, I am not patient in processing an issue. Recognizing shortcomings can help to mitigate them, and seeing them both in myself and my dad has helped me to recognize a pattern. As he would be quick to say, leadership lessons come not only in our successes but also through our failures.

Moreover, it is not just my father from whom I have learned lessons of leadership. My mother has an uncanny ability to be present with people, asking questions that encourage transparency and confidence. She is also very at ease with herself, which makes her at ease with others. She can meet the president and first lady, or a young mother in a Bible study, and be equally at home in each social situation. She has been a model for me in how to relate to a great diversity of people. She is not perfect either, and I sometimes share with her an anxiety about the world and about those we love.

We don't get to choose our parents, so I am deeply grateful to God for the parents whom He gave me, for they have been a deep and abiding blessing in my life. I appreciate the many ways that they have shaped the person whom I have become. Indeed, a childhood friend of mine once described me as a person who has the "work engine of his father and the soft skills of his mother," a description that, if true, is a great compliment. Their steadfast example of faith in Christ has been their greatest gift to me, and it is the most important thing that I have tried to pass along to my children. Christ is the One Who orients me in my work, Who energizes me in my community, Who forgives me when I fall short, Who sustains me in life's greatest sorrows, and Who died and rose again so that I may have life. I have come from a family of faith, and that is the greatest gift that I could have received.

I received these stories of leadership as part of the normal conversations around our dining room table. In writing this book, Dad has given other people the opportunity to eavesdrop on those conversations. I trust that, as you have listened to those conversations, you have been encouraged to lead with joy, serve in love, and follow in faith.

Notes

(Numbers refer to pages where referenced material appears.)

Introduction

17 "All the world's a stage . . ." William Shakespeare, *As You Like It*, act 2, scene 7.

20 "There is a tide in the affairs of men . . ." William Shakespeare, *Julius Caesar*, act 4, scene 3.

Chapter 1

23 "Midnight Games," an unpublished version of a poem by Gordon MacDonald. Used with permission. A modified version appears in *When Men Think Private Thoughts* (Nashville: Thomas Nelson, 1996), xi.

36 "Something which . . . appears in me . . ." C. S. Lewis, *Mere Christianity* (New York: HarperOne, 2009), 25.

36 "All the human beings . . ." C. S. Lewis, *The Problem of Pain* (New York: HarperOne, 2001), 10.

37 "Virtue . . . brings light . . ." Lewis, *Mere Christianity*, 102.

37 Armand M. Nicholi, *The Question of God: C. S. Lewis and Sigmund Freud Debate God, Love, Sex, and the Meaning of Life* (New York: Free Press, 2002).

39 "I am not examining the case . . ." Alexander I. Solzhenitsyn, *A World Split Apart: Commencement Address Delivered at Harvard University, June 8, 1978* (New York: Harper & Row, 1978), 55–57, 59–61.

40 "The ideology [of Communism] disappears completely . . ." Aleksandr Solzhenitsyn, interview by Georges Suffert, *Encounter* (April 1976), quoted in John B. Dunlop, Richard S. Haugh, and Michael Nicholson, eds., *Solzhenitsyn in Exile: Critical Essays and Documentary Materials* (Stanford, CA: Hoover Institution Press, 1985), 262.

40 "Who stands fast? Only the man . . ." Dietrich Bonhoeffer, *Letters and Papers from Prison*, ed. Eberhard Bethge (New York: Simon & Schuster, 1997), 5.

41 "Management is, by itself, a liberal art. . . ." Peter Drucker, "What Have I Learned? A Look Back and a Look Ahead," draft of speech delivered at Claremont Graduate University, Oct. 21, 1987.

42 Joseph A. Maciariello and Karen E. Linkletter, *Drucker's Lost Art of Management: Peter Drucker's Timeless Vision for Building Effective Organizations* (New York: McGraw-Hill, 2011), 33–41, 107–21.

42 "Human existence is possible . . ." Peter Drucker, "The Unfashionable Kierkegaard," *Sewanee Review* 57:4 (Fall 1949): 587–602.

48 "I came about like a well-handled ship." Robert Louis Stevenson, cited in Bradford Torrey, "Robert Louis Stevenson," review of *The Life of Robert Louis Stevenson*, by Graham Balfour, *Atlantic Monthly* (June 1902), http://www.theatlantic.com/past/docs/unbound/classrev/rlsteve.htm.

Chapter 2

49 "Leap of faith." Part of headline on a story about Jeremy Lin. "Leap of Faith Launched New Star," *USA Today*, Feb. 17, 2012.

50 "Everyone who thinks this is an overnight success . . ." Jeff Zillgitt, "How Did Every-

one Miss Jeremy Lin?" *USA Today*, Feb. 17, 2012, http://usatoday30.usatoday.com/sports/basketball/nba/story/2012-02-15/how-did-everyone-miss-jeremy-lin/53124082/1.

50 "I want to be the same person . . ." Ibid.

58 C. William Pollard, *The Soul of the Firm* (New York: HarperBusiness; Grand Rapids: Zondervan, 1996).

59 W. Edwards Deming on our inborn curiosity, point made in speech heard by the author.

66 Joel I. Klein, Condoleezza Rice, and Julia Levy, *U.S. Education Reform and National Security* (New York: Council on Foreign Relations, Independent Task Force, 2012). http://i.cfr.org/content/publications/attachments/TFR68_Education_National_Security.pdf.

74 "It may be possible to make the world more tolerable . . ." Peter Drucker, comment made in personal conversation with the author.

79 "[God] could, if He chose . . ." C. S. Lewis, "The Efficacy of Prayer," in *The World's Last Night and Other Essays* (New York: Harcourt, Brace, 1960), 9.

81 "A careful man I want to be . . ." Author unknown.

Chapter 3

87 ". . . a way of life in which the nature of man . . ." Dorothy L. Sayers, "Why Work?" in *Creed or Chaos?* (Manchester, NH: Sophia Institute Press, 1995), 63.

88 "A housemaid who does her work . . ." Martin Luther, cited in Brian Watts, *The Treasure in the Field* (Langley, BC: Imogen Resources, 1995), 178, http://treasureinthefield.org/Treasure%20in%20the%20Field.pdf.

88 Regarding John Calvin's view of work, see John Calvin, *Institutes of the Christian Religion*, ed. John T. McNeill and trans. Ford Lewis Battles (Philadelphia: Westminster Press, 1960), 724–25.

88 "Gain all you can." John Wesley, "The Use of Money," *Sermons on Several Occasions*, Sermon 50, *Christian Classics Ethereal Library*, http://www.ccel.org/ccel/wesley/sermons.v.l.html.

89 Max Weber, *The Protestant Ethic and the Spirit of Capitalism*, trans. Talcott Parsons (Mineola, NY: Dover, 2003), 181–82.

89 "Can men live in a free society . . ." George Gilder, *Wealth and Poverty: A New Edition for the Twenty-First Century* (Washington, DC: Regnery, 2012), 7.

90 Robert S. Michaelsen, "The American Gospel of Work and the Protestant Doctrine of Vocation" (unpublished PhD dissertation, Yale University, 1951).

91 ". . . primarily, a thing one does to live . . ." Sayers, "Why Work?" 73.

95 "There are no *ordinary* people. . . ." C. S. Lewis, *The Weight of Glory and Other Addresses* (New York: HarperOne, 2001), 46. Emphasis added.

97 "Enemies within." Kenneth Labich, "Why Companies Fail," *Fortune* magazine, November 14, 1994, http://money.cnn.com/magazines/fortune/fortune_archive/1994/11/14/79957/index.htm.

99 Joseph A. Schumpeter, "The Process of Creative Destruction," in *Capitalism, Socialism and Democracy*, 3rd ed. (New York: Harper, 1976), 81–86.

99 "We have arrived at this point . . ." "Obama Remarks on the Economy," *The Wall Street Journal*, January 9, 2009, http://blogs.wsj.com/economics/2009/01/08/obama-remarks-on-the-economy/.

101 ". . . like building model airplanes . . ." Stephen L. Carter, *The Culture of Disbelief: How American Law and Politics Trivialize Religious Devotion* (New York: BasicBooks, 1993), 22.

102 David W. Miller, *God at Work: The History and Promise of the Faith at Work Movement* (Oxford: Oxford University Press, 2007), especially 80–89.

107 "There is little hope for democracy . . ." Margaret Thatcher, "Speech to General Assembly of the Church of Scotland," May 21, 1988, Assembly Hall, The Mound, Edinburgh. http://www.margaretthatcher.org/document/107246.

108 "When the Stranger says . . ." T. S. Eliot, "Choruses from 'The Rock,'" in *The Complete Poems and Plays, 1909–1950* (San Diego: Harcourt Brace Jovanovich, 1971), 103.

Chapter 4

109 "Two roads diverged in a yellow wood . . ." Robert Frost, "The Road Not Taken," in *Collected Poems, Prose, & Plays* (New York: Library of America, 1995), 103.

Chapter 5

125 "A leader has only one choice . . ." Peter Drucker, comment made in personal conversation with the author.

128 Max De Pree, *Leadership Jazz: The Essential Elements of a Great Leader*, rev. ed. (New York: Doubleday, 2008), 17.

135 "For many people who don't know the folks at ServiceMaster . . ." and "ServiceMaster has achieved such adherence to its values . . ." Noel M. Tichy and Eli Cohen, *The Leadership Engine: How Winning Companies Build Leaders at Every Level* (New York: HarperBusiness, 1997), 109–11. The quotation from C. William Pollard is found in *The Soul of the Firm* (Grand Rapids: Zondervan, 1996), 20.

138 "A dead corpse doesn't smell any better . . ." Peter Drucker, *Management Challenges for the 21st Century* (New York: HarperBusiness, 2001), 75.

140 "You have many critics . . ." C. S. Lewis, cited in Walter Hooper, *C. S. Lewis: A Complete Guide to His Life & Works* (New York: HarperCollins, 1998), 76.

Chapter 6

147 Joseph A. Schumpeter, "The Process of Creative Destruction," in *Capitalism, Socialism and Democracy*, 3rd ed. (New York: Harper, 1976), 81–86.

148 Adam Smith, *An Inquiry into the Nature and Causes of the Wealth of Nations*, ed. Edwin Cannan (1776; repr., New York: Modern Library, 1994), 485.

150 Max Weber, *The Protestant Ethic and the Spirit of Capitalism*, trans. Talcott Parsons (Mineola, NY: Dover, 2003), 181–2.

152 Robert William Fogel, *The Fourth Great Awakening & the Future of Egalitarianism* (Chicago: University of Chicago Press, 2000).

153 Benjamin M. Friedman, *The Moral Consequences of Economic Growth* (New York: Knopf, 2005).

154 Steve Kroft, *60 Minutes* interview with George Soros, Dec. 20, 1998.

158 George Carey and Andrew Carey, *We Don't Do God* (Oxford: Monarch Books, 2012).

158 Greg Forster, "Greed Is Not Good for Capitalism," The Gospel Coalition (blog), August 15, 2012, http://thegospelcoalition.org/blogs/tgc/2012/08/15/greed-is-not-good -for-capitalism/.

172 Peter Drucker on developing human character. C. William Pollard and Donald D. Holt, eds., *The Heart of a Business Ethic* (Lanham, MD: University Press of America, 2005).

Chapter 7

177 "Change is the law of life. . . ." John F. Kennedy, "Address in the Assembly Hall at the Paulskirche in Frankfurt," June 25, 1963, *The American Presidency Project*, http://www .presidency.ucsb.edu/ws/?pid=9303#axzz2iSet4NtW.

181 "There are no ordinary people. . . ." C. S. Lewis, *The Weight of Glory and Other Addresses* (New York: HarperOne, 2001), 46.

183 Ranking as #1 service company, *Fortune* magazine, June 5, 1989.

183 Description as "star of the future," *The Wall Street Journal*, June 23, 1987.

183 *Financial Times* ranking. Cited in James L. Heskett, *The Culture Cycle: How to Shape the Unseen Force That Transforms Performance* (Upper Saddle River, NJ: FT Press, 2012), 70.

184 Layers of management as relay switches. Peter Drucker, "The Coming of the New Organization," Harvard Business Review, January 1988, br.org/1988/01/the-coming-of-the-new-organization/ar/1.

186 "Yesterday's breadwinners." Peter Drucker, *Classic Drucker: Essential Wisdom of Peter Drucker from the Pages of* Harvard Business Review (Boston: Harvard Business Press, 2006), 93.

187 "A dead corpse doesn't smell any better . . ." Peter Drucker, *Management Challenges for the 21st Century* (New York: HarperBusiness, 2001), 75.

187 Heskett, *The Culture Cycle: How to Shape the Unseen Force That Transforms Performance.*

193 "A leader has only one choice . . ." Peter Drucker, comment made in personal conversation with the author.

Chapter 8

195 "What life have you if you have not life together? . . ." T. S. Eliot, "Choruses from 'The Rock,'" in *The Complete Poems and Plays, 1909–1950* (San Diego: Harcourt Brace Jovanovich, 1971), 101–3.

196 C. S. Lewis, "Learning in War-Time," in *The Weight of Glory and Other Addresses* (New York: HarperOne, 2001), 47–63.

203 "People work for a cause." Peter Drucker, cited in Keith Harrell, *The Attitude of Leadership: Taking the Lead and Keeping It* (Hoboken, NJ: John Wiley & Sons, 2003), 166.

204 "The first requirement [of a board member] is competence." Peter Drucker, "Needed: An Effective Board," in *Management: Tasks, Responsibilities, Practices* (New York: Harper & Row, 1973), 635.

205 Information on the Sarbanes-Oxley legislation can be found at the web site of the U.S. Securities and Exchange Commission, http://www.sec.gov/about/laws.shtml #sox2002.

207 Max De Pree, *Leadership Is an Art* (New York: Doubleday, 1989), 81.

209 ". . . do all business that may be necessary and appropriate . . ." Wheaton College Charter, sec. 3, Wheaton College Archives & Special Collections, http://espace .wheaton.edu/lr/a-sc/archives/blanchard/CollegeCharter18610228-mss.pdf.

209 Billy Graham among most-admired people. Jeffrey M. Jones, "Obama, Clinton Continue Reign as Most Admired," *Gallup Politics*, December 31, 2013, http://www.gallup .com/poll/166646/obama-clinton-continue-reign-admired-man-woman.aspx.

213 "Pollard has an unusual knack . . ." *Director's Alert: Corporate America's Outstanding Directors 1999*, 19.

220 "Where is the life we have lost in living . . ." Eliot, "Choruses from 'The Rock,'" in *The Complete Poems and Plays*, 96, 100.

Chapter 9

221 "In succession houses rise and fall . . ." T. S. Eliot, "East Coker," *Four Quartets*, in *The Complete Poems and Plays, 1909–1950* (San Diego: Harcourt Brace Jovanovich, 1971), 123–29.

239 Brian Oxley, *The Last Tower* (Naperville, IL: OxVision Books, a division of BridgePoint International, LLC, 2012).

243 Joseph A. Maciariello and Karen E. Linkletter, *Drucker's Lost Art of Management: Peter Drucker's Timeless Vision for Building Effective Organizations* (New York: McGraw-Hill, 2011).

243 James L. Heskett, *The Culture Cycle: How to Shape the Unseen Force That Transforms Performance* (Upper Saddle River, NJ: FT Press, 2012).

252 David W. Miller, *God at Work: The History and Promise of the Faith at Work Movement* (New York: Oxford University Press, 2007).

253 Peter Drucker on management as a liberal art. See quotation on 41–42.

256 "An old man going a lone highway . . ." Will Allen Dromgoole, "The Bridge Builder," in Margery Doud and Cleo M. Parsley, eds., *Father: An Anthology of Verse* (New York: E. P. Dutton, 1931), 86.

Index